Harmonic Numerology

The Numerology
of the
Pythagoreans

Gene F. Collins Jr., Ph.D.

ISBN-10: 1460981677
ISBN-13: 978-1460981672

This book was printed in the United States of America.

To order books or for customer service, please call 1-309-713-2667.
drgfcollins@yahoo.com
www.cosmopsychology.com

Dedication

To my mother Edna Jacqueline Collins

I dedicate this book to my parents Gene Frank Collins, Sr. and Edna Jacqueline Collins and my grandparents Everett E. King, Edna M. King, Leroy Collins, and Ruth Geraldine Collins, who have been there through thick and thin and encouraged me throughout my journey.

And to those everywhere who actualize the great mother archetype
y many teachers, friends, and clients who have shared their knowledge, wisdom, and lives with me.

Table of Contents

Numerology
The Science of Numbers
Chapter 1

Teach us to number our days aright,
that we may gain a heart of wisdom.
Psalm 90:12

God writes the Gospel not in the Bible alone,
but also on trees,
and in the flowers and clouds and stars.
Martin Luther

Vibrations, reach on up to become light,
And then through gamma, out of sight.
Between the eyes and ears there lie,
The sounds of color and the light of a sigh.
And to hear the sun, what a thing to believe,
But it's all around if we could but perceive.
To know ultra-violet, infra-red, and x-rays,
Beauty to find in so many ways.
Graeme Edge

Numerology is the study of the occult meanings of numbers and their significance in human life. It is the use of numbers to determine the nature or quality of any person, place, thing, event, or process, whether in the present, past, or future. Numerology is a self-help tool that can be used to gain insights into your character and personality. It describes the patterns and cycles that underlie the events of your life. It reveals your strengths and weaknesses as they ebb and flow throughout your life. It also reveals the psychological dilemmas, the karmic lessons, and the spiritual meanings at each point of your journey.

Of all the metaphysical sciences, numerology is the simplest to understand and use. Unlike astrology, you do not need the precision and exactness of birth data, of longitude and latitude, a table of houses, or the complicated mathematical calculations that are required for an astrological chart. You do not need a professional reader, or years of intensive study, or intuitive or psychic development required in astrology, cartomancy, palmistry, or graphology. (Admittedly, a little native intuitive or psychic ability would be helpful, though.)

All you need to know is a given name at birth, a birthdate, and some simple addition and subtraction skills. Through numerology, it is possible to determine what numbers are active in your life, what numbers signify your blessings, and what numbers challenge you to grow beyond who you think you are. Numerology can help you learn how to best use your abilities, talents, and skills to live day-by-day in ways that are personally fulfilling and spiritually meaningful.

To the numerologist, all of the hustle and bustle of this modern world can be reduced to the numbers that stand behind the appearances. Using only the date of birth and one's given name (as recorded on the birth certificate), those numbers that represent one's particular life forces can be determined. Numerology reveals a great deal about one's character, one's purpose in life, motivations, and talents and abilities. Numerology can be used to get in touch with one's inner most feelings, to recognize vocational tendencies, to accomplish goals, and to make important life decisions.

Numerology is especially useful for understanding significant relationships and for determining compatibilities. It can be used to guide the course of one's life so that actions are in harmony with, and supported by, the forces at work in each person's unique destiny. Numerology can be used to know when to move forward in the pursuit of happiness and when to wait for a more favorable time. Numerology can be used to determine the best time for any major life activity.

Numerology has been used to decide when to invest, when to marry, when to travel, when to change jobs, or when to relocate. Numerology reveals truths without having to resort to the use of extra-sensory perception and related psychic abilities. However, the practice of numerology does benefit from a well-developed sense of intuition, and it is at its best when used in conjunction with psychic sensitivities of ESP.

Everything in the universe can be described by a set of mathematical relationships. The numerologist believes that everything in universe can be understood by numbers that describe their underlying energies. Knowledge of the numbers that underlie a name, date, etc. provides an understanding of the particular person, place, or thing described by the numbers. At any time during our life we are working with several different numbers.

When these numbers are understood in the context of the world around us, certain trends and opportunities become clear. Numerologists believe that every person is totally unique and that, in accordance with cosmic law, everyone is born at a particular time and place and given a distinct name so that he or she can continue to grow on his or her particular path.

Numerology is an ancient practice and one of the oldest of the metaphysical sciences and techniques of divination. No one knows when numerology was first used to describe human nature or forecast future events, but there is evidence that numerology was practiced as long ago as 3100 BC. The ancient Egyptians, Chaldeans, Babylonians, Assyrians, and Hebrews all used some form of numerology. We know that numerology was practiced as well by the Arabs, the Chinese, the Christians, the Druids, the Essenes, the Incas, the Japanese, the Mayans, and the Phoenicians. It is believed that every primitive culture used some form of numerology.

Pythagoras of Samos

Philosophy flourished in Ancient Greece. The ancient Greek philosopher Pythagoras of Samos (c. 570 BC - c. 495 BC) became known as the father of Western philosophy, numerology, mathematics, geometry, and music. Pythagoras was the founder of wave theory in general and of acoustics—the science of mechanical waves—in particular. He discovered the properties of vibrating strings, which he described as ratios of integers that produced the harmonic overtone series. He established the meaning of numbers and became the founder of Western numerology.

Pythagoras lived at approximately the same time that Prince Siddhartha Gautama (c. 563 - 483 BC) was establishing Buddhism in India and that Lao-Tzu (6th century BC) wrote the Tao Te Ching (The Canon of the Way and the Power) and was establishing Taoism in China. Confucius (551 – 479 BC) was establishing his philosophy of social order in China at this time as well.

Pythagoras traveled around the eastern coast of the Mediterranean Sea and established the Order of the Pythagoreans--a university or mystery school of higher learning. Because of Pythagoras' intense desire to understand the nature of the universe, he was the first person to call himself a Lover of Wisdom or philosopher. Pythagoras eventually became the high priest of the temple of Delphi.

Pythagoras taught that the Earth was round and possibly revolved around the Sun. By the time of the Roman Empire, his heliocentric theory of the solar system was "disproven." However, his theory regarding the celestial music created by the planets was "proven" or "accepted."

Most of our information concerning of numerology originated with Pythagoras. He assembled the various resources on numerology available at the time and organized and crafted the practice of numerology into one of its most popular forms used today. He believed that all things could be expressed in numerical terms and ultimately reduced to numbers. He taught that all things in the universe were created through numbers, that numbers were divine archetypes, and that every number had its own meaning and nature. Everything in the observable universe could be reduced to or described by numbers.

Numbers symbolized the stages that an idea in the mind of God must pass through in order to become a physical reality. Every number stood for a particular stage of being and represented the nature or meaning of that particular stage. Numbers were considered to be archetypes or spiritual ideas, each having its own meaning on the ideal or spiritual planes of existence and each seeking to manifest itself in the material world. Since numbers and mathematics serve all sciences, numerology was given the title Mother of Sciences.

Pythagoras is considered to be a father of modern geometry. He discovered the mathematical laws of regular polygons and the Pythagorean theorem regarding triangles. He discovered the diatonic (musical) scale used today.

Pythagoras is also considered to be a father of harmonics--the study of musical sound. While playing the lyre, he noticed that he could create the different harmonics by placing his finger at fractional points on the string. Where he placed his finger corresponded to the nodes of each harmonic. Pythagoras discovered that a harmonic of a wave is a component frequency of the wave that is created by dividing the original frequency by integers—the numbers 1, 2, 3, 4, etc.

Pythagoras hypothesized that, like the lyre, music was produced by the distance between the planets of the solar system. He discovered correspondences among numbers, music, shapes, and planets.

Pythagoras' theory--that all things could be described ultimately by numbers--became the basis of the physical sciences of today such as biology, chemistry, physics, geology, and astronomy. His theory that every number is a meaningful archetype which bestows its meaning upon whatever object it creates, is the basis of numerology, astrology, palmistry, and color and musical healing. Most metaphysical subjects find their way back to Pythagoras.

Socrates

The Greek philosopher Socrates (c. 469 BC – c. 399 BC) was one of the most famous and influential founders of Western philosophy. I am mentioning Socrates because of his contributions to Western philosophy, metaphysics, and esotericism and because he served as the bridge between Pythagoras and Plato.

Socrates made significant contributions in the philosophical fields of ethics, logic, metaphysics, and epistemology. Like Siddhartha and Jesus, he left it to his students to record his teachings. Little is known about his life outside of what they wrote. His most famous student Plato referred to him extensively in his writings. The stories of Socrates tell us that he was wrongfully found guilty of corrupting the minds of the youth of Athens and for this was executed by drinking hemlock.

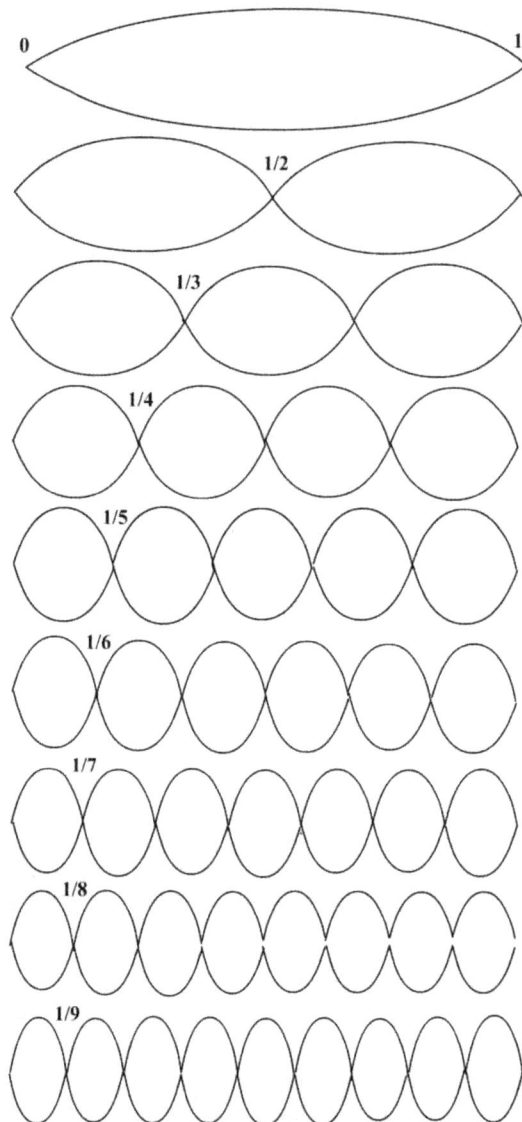

Harmonic Waves
The First through Ninth Harmonics

Socrates is probably most well-known for his unusual method of teaching, referred to as the *Socratic method*. When asked a question by one of his students, Socrates asked the student questions which led the student to the answer. Socrates believed that the soul had access to all knowledge prior to birth in a physical body and that by questioning oneself that knowledge could be retrieved. Socrates is also known for the *Socratic paradoxes* which included questions regarding knowledge and evil.

According to Plato, Socrates considered the soul to be the essence of a human being. Socrates believed that our souls made our decisions and directed our actions. He further believed that the soul was incorporeal and eternal. Our physical bodies die, but our souls are continually reborn in subsequent bodies.

The Socratic-Platonic conception of the soul consists of three parts: the *logos*, the *thymos*, and the *eros*. The logos is the center that best corresponds to the mind or nous. The logos uses reason and logic to direct and balance the thymos and the eros. The thymos is the center of egocentric emotions or spiritedness. The thymos is the source of emotions which lead to acts of bravery and to the pursuit of fame and glory. If unchecked by the logos, the emotions of the thymos lead to pride and arrogance. The eros is the source of desires and appetites. The eros provides the thrust to fulfill basic physical needs. If unchecked by the logos, the passions of the eros lead to a life of hedonism. Inner peace is experienced when the logos regulates and balances the functions of the thymos and eros.

Plato

The Greek philosopher Plato (427 BC - 347 BC) was our primary source of information on the life and teachings of his teacher Socrates. Plato was also our major source concerning the legend of Atlantis. As a member of the Order of the Pythagoreans, Plato taught the Pythagorean theory of numerology. He expanded the Pythagorean meaning of numbers to geometric shapes in his theory of forms. According to Plato, the universe consists of cosmic vibrations of varying frequencies and amplitudes. These vibrations were contained within the infinite mind or intelligence of God. They formed the basic units of force or meaning underlying all manifest or objective reality. The cosmic vibrations were constantly changing in measurable and predictable ways which could be described by numbers. Plato taught that each planet symbolized a particular tone or frequency and that together the planets produced a harmonious musical chorus. Plato referred to this phenomenon as the *music of the spheres*.

Plato referred to the above concept of God and the universe as *idealism*. In Plato's idealism: 1) God is the only reality; 2) God is eternal; 3) God is both ever-changing and never-changing; 4) multiplicity or the existence of separate objects is false; 5) God is a mental-spiritual field filled with ideas *(eidos)*; 6) ideas *(eidos)* manifest as objective, physical reality; 7) physical reality is an illusion and the senses constitute the source of all illusion and error; and 8) physical reality can be manipulated through the proper use of mental-spiritual ideas *(eidos)* and self-discipline.

Plato called his theory of idealism the *theory of forms*. According to Plato, human reason apprehends immutable, eternal, unchanging forms called *eidos*. *Eideos* (Greek for *visual figures, shapes,* or *forms*) are abstract, transcendental, and universal. Particular things in the realm of appearance represent or reflect *eidos*. Particular things, such as flowers, the human body, clouds, water, mountains, etc., are judged by how well they represent their particular *eido*. The more similar the thing is to its corresponding *eido*, the more beautiful it is judged. Human beings are able to perceive the world of eternal forms or *eidos* by means of the *nous*, the rational part of the mind. Plato also believed that this same *nous* was the only immortal part of the soul.

After Plato

As part of the philosophy and culture of ancient Greece, Pythagorean numerology continued to survive in Europe until the Age of Reason in the 18th century AD. However, due to the new philosophies of exoteric Christianity, numerology began to lose its status in Europe at the height of the Roman Empire. At the First Council of Nicaea in 325 AD, interest in sacred numbers and the practice of numerology were no longer accepted by the Christian Church. The numerological symbolism in the Bible became the property of esoteric Christianity.

Pythagoreans taught that the Earth was a rotating sphere revolving around a central fire. With the fall of the Roman Empire and the beginning of the Dark Ages in Europe, the powerful leaders in the Christian church banned the teaching of Pythagoras' beliefs. The Christian leaders insisted that the Judeo-Christian Bible taught that the Sun orbited the Earth. Anyone who adhered to the ideas of Pythagoras was tortured and/or killed.

Long after Pythagoras, the German astrologer Johannes Kepler (1571 AD – 1630 AD) related Plato's forms and shapes to solids, planets, and planetary aspects in his theory of the celestial music of polyphony. The astrologer Nicolaus Copernicus (1473-1543) also determined that the Earth revolved around the Sun, but his heliocentric cosmology went largely unnoticed until Galileo started disseminating the ideas of Pythagoras and Copernicus. Just before the Renaissance, church leaders were still forcing famous astrologers, such as Galileo, to recant publicly the teachings of Pythagoras.

The sciences of today are as dependent on numbers as were the metaphysical sciences throughout the ages. However, today's scientists use numbers as measurements and do not interpret the spiritual idea represented by numbers. Today's orthodox scientists recognize the importance of numbers and mathematics, but they do not acknowledge the metaphysical tenets of numerology.

The popularity of subjects like numerology began to rise again with the Romantic Movement of the in the second half of the 18th century in Europe. Numerology became a household term during the New Age Movement of the 1960s

Schools of Numerology

The practice of numerology all but disappeared as the Age of Enlightenment began in Europe. Numerology went underground and became an esoteric and an occult science or practice. Numerology resurfaced in the late 1800's as did the other metaphysical sciences. Like the others, numerology has experienced a resurge in popularity. There are currently three Western schools of numerology—the Pythagorean, the Chaldean, and the Kabbalistic systems. Vedic numerology and Chinese numerology are the most popular Asian systems. Every system has some distinctly different features and offers a unique perspective. However, the systems are far more similar than they are different. In particular, all systems provide the same interpretations of each number. The Pythagorean system is probably the most popular today, but all systems are in use and can be used together to provide rich, multi-leveled interpretations.

The three most popular schools of Western numerology are the Chaldean, the Kabalistic, and the Pythagorean. Other very popular schools of numerology include Vedic, or Indian, numerology and some forms of Chinese and Japanese numerology. For the most part, the three Western forms of numerology and Vedic numerology assign the same or very similar meanings to each number. There is some variation regarding secondary associations, such as which planet goes with which number. Chinese systems differ more in regards to the meanings assigned to each number and emphasize good or lucky numbers and bad or unlucky numbers.

In Vedic numerology there is some consideration of good or lucky numbers and bad or unlucky numbers. Vedic numerology did not experience the degree of cultural and religious rejection that was displayed by Christianity and scientism in the West. Vedic numerology remains well connected with the rest of its culture. For example, Vedic numerology can be used to diagnose and treat physical or medical conditions.

The Chaldean system of numerology is probably of oldest of the three Western forms and was originally developed in Ancient Babylon. Chaldean numerology begins by substituting the numbers *1* through *8* for the letters of the name and the birthdate. Chaldean numerology views the number *9* as very sacred or holy and does not use it when first changing letters into numbers. However, if a sum of numbers adds up to *9*, the *9* is included in the numerological reading and is interpreted as an indication of divine intercession. Additionally, Chaldean numerology does not reduce all numbers to single digits and master numbers. Double digits are not reduced to single digits. Sums that add up to single digits refer to inner qualities, and those that add up to double digits refer to outer characteristics.

Kabalistic numerology begins by substituting the numbers *1* through *22*, in accordance with the *22* letters of the Hebrew alphabet for the letters of the name. It has been modified slightly to accommodate the Roman alphabet. The birthdate is not normally used in Kabalistic numerology.

The Chaldean Method							
1	2	3	4	5	6	7	8
A	B	C	D	E	U	O	F
I	K	G	M	H	V	Z	P
J	R	L	T	N	W		
Q		S		X			
Y							

Pythagorean numerology begins by substituting the numbers *1* through *9* for the letters in the name. Pythagorean numerology uses the birthdate and reduces all numbers to single digits or master numbers. Most numerologists use *11* and *22* as master numbers. A few use *33*, and even fewer use *44* as a master number. Some numerologists do not use master numbers at all. From the name and birthdate, several numbers are calculated that describe behavioral, psychological, and spiritual dispositions. Additionally, several numbers are calculated that are used to describe future trends and possible events.

The Pythagorean Method								
1	2	3	4	5	6	7	8	9
A	B	C	D	E	F	G	H	I
J	K	L	M	N	O	P	Q	R
S	T	U	V	W	X	Y	Z	

Numbers
Their Symbolic Meanings
Chapter 2

Every natural fact is a symbol of some spiritual fact.
Ralph Waldo Emerson

Every phenomenon of nature was a word, -
the sign, symbol and pledge of a new, mysterious, inexpressible
but all the more intimate union, participation
and community of divine energies and ideas.
Johann G. Hamann

Each number has a distinctive vibration.
Lloyd Cope

When you have mastered numbers,
you will in fact no longer be reading numbers,
any more than you read words when reading books.
You will be reading meanings.
W. E. B. Du Bois

Learning and applying numerology involves three stages or phases—learning the meaning of the numbers, calculating the various personal number values, and finally synthesizing these values into a meaningful portrait or numeroscope. This chapter is about the first—learning the symbolic or qualitative meaning of the numbers. Once you learn these symbolic values, you can apply their meanings to number expressions of the numeroscope. These meanings can also be applied to astrology, cartomancy, and metaphysics in general. They can be applied in the course of your daily life to discover the underlying purpose of whatever event is occurring or whatever activity you are performing.

In numerology, numbers have both a quantitative and a qualitative meaning. Most people are used to working with the quantitative aspect of numbers. For example, the quantitative meaning of the number "1" is one thing. The quantitative meaning of the number "2" is two things, and so on. Numerology uses the quantitative meaning of numbers in order to combine numbers in dates, names, addresses, etc.

After working with the quantitative meanings, numerology applies the qualitative meanings of the numbers. The qualitative meaning of the number "1" refers to the nature of oneness—the special qualities that pertain to oneness. The qualitative meaning of the number "2" refers to the particular qualities of being a two or of "two-ness." And so on with 3, 4, etc. Most everyone has an unconscious or intuitive grasp of the qualitative aspect of numbers, but very few people think about these meanings consciously. In this day and age, it is unheard of for children to be taught the qualitative meanings of numbers in school. Believe it or not, this was not always true. During the

Middle Ages in Europe, the qualitative meaning of numbers was a fundamental part of a liberal education. Such knowledge was considered to be essential in order to understand the Bible properly. The qualitative aspect of numbers formed the foundation of the *eidos* of classical Greek philosophy. Today such meanings are found only in books on numerology, astrology, and similar occult subjects, where numbers refer to the steps or stages of a process.

Just like the zodiac, every number symbolizes a step in the process of creation. The first step is symbolized by the number one. The second step is symbolized by the number two, and so on. For example, if the numbers of a particular day add up to the number three, you know that this day favors the third step in whatever process you are engaged. If the address of a building you are in adds up to the number five, you know that this building favors the fifth step of any process. If you encounter someone whose name adds up to the number eight, you know that the energies of this person favor the eighth step of any process.

In numerology, every point in the universe, the infinite mind, or divine intelligence has access to information regarding all other points regardless of distance in space and time (past, present, and future). This information is contained in the archetypes of numbers, which are only partially comprehensible to humans. Knowledge of the number archetypes allows a person to align his or her will and ego with the purposes of the universe. Knowledge of number archetypes may also allow one to participate in and direct the ongoing processes of the universe or of his or her life.

Interpretation by the Numbers

The meanings for the numbers *1* through *10*, *0*, and the master numbers *11*, *22*, *33*, and *44* are given below, accompanied by personality traits and behaviors commonly associated with each number. Where applicable, the Pythagorean meanings and associated geometric shapes are given. Also where applicable, the planets, urges, and elements of C. C. Zain's esoteric psychology and the crises and resulting personal power of Erik H. Erikson's identity development are included. In general, odd numbers are masculine, active, and positive. Even numbers are feminine, receptive, and negative.

Number 1

Individuality, Purpose

Pythagorean numerology begins with the number *1*. Called the *monad*, *1* is represented by a point. It is the source of all numbers, the origin of all things. It symbolizes the primal state of unity, indivisibility, and oneness. Some say that it is both an odd and an even number. The *1* is the number of God, the Prime Masculine Number, and the Yang. It manifests as the active principle, the number of consciousness, light, the ego, the father, and authority. The Pythagoreans considered *1* to be good, desirable, essential, and indivisible. The *1* is associated with the Sun, fire, and the colors red and red-orange.

Wherever the *1* is found in the numeroscope, it indicates the beginning of a new cycle, beginnings in general, creation, individuality, and selfhood. In esoteric psychology, the *1* signifies the Sun and the power urges, i.e., the desire to survive and to be something. In identity development, the *1* signifies the *trust versus mistrust crisis* from which arises the power of *hope.*

Personality traits and behaviors associated with *1* include: adventure, aggressiveness, aloneness, ambition, arrogance, assertiveness, bossiness, confidence, courage, creativity, desire, determination, dignity, direction, dominant, egotism, egotistical, false pride, independence, individualism, individuality, initiative, intolerance, leadership, loneliness, masculinity, newness, obstinate, optimism, originality, pioneering, pomposity, powerful, prestige, resistance, self-assurance, self-centeredness, selfishness, solitariness, strength, tyrannical, and willpower.

Number 2

Polarity, Union

The number *2* is called the *dyad* and is represented by a line. It indicates the loss of the primal unity. The *2* is duality, and the Pythagoreans believed that *2* is a number of excess, the first feminine number, and a defective number. The *2* represents the principles of matter, manifestation, and material evolution. The *1* has been separated into *2*. With the *2*, a new relationship is now possible. Something has been created which is external of the *1*. *2* is both the forming of dichotomies, the division of things into two categories, and the initial emergence of life. Awareness of the other creates tension and makes union and partnership possible. The *2* is the prime feminine number, the number of polarities, pairs, partners, opposites, and antithesis. The *2* is associated with the Moon, water, the oceans, and the color orange. Sometimes *2* is associated with blue.

Wherever *2* is found in the numeroscope, it indicates externalization, separation, tension, conflict, union, partnership, cooperation, rhythm, attachment, nurturing, femininity, and motherhood. In esoteric psychology, the *2* signifies the Moon and the domestic elements of self-preservation and race preservation. In identity development, the *2* signifies the *autonomy versus shame and self-doubt crisis* from which arises the power of *will.*

Personality traits and behaviors associated with *2* include: absorption, adaptability, apathy, appeasement, attachment, awareness, balance, bonding, caution, conflict, cooperation, cruelty, deceit, dependence, diplomacy, emotions, empathy, expedience, feelings, females, femininity, fluctuation, friendship, gentleness, home, instinct, intuition, hypersensitivity, kindness, maliciousness, marriage, mediation, motherhood, neediness, nurturing, obedience, parental, partnership, patience, peace-making, pettiness, petulance, reaction, receptivity, relationship, rhythm, self-consciousness, self-effacement, self-sacrifice, sensitivity, separation, shyness, submissiveness, tension, touchiness, understanding, union, and withdrawal.

Number 3

Interaction, Synthesis

The number *3* is referred to as the *triad*. It is represented by a plane, is composed of unity and diversity, and restores them to harmony. It is the first odd, masculine number. The *3* is the principle of spirit and the process of spiritual evolution through reconciliation of opposites by finding common elements or points of agreement. The *3* is the process of synthesis. The *3* represents the trinity or triune god found in most religions. The *1* is the thesis, the *2* is the antithesis, and the *3* is the synthesis. The *3* harmonizes dichotomies and is considered to be an extremely lucky number. It is ease, flow, grace, happiness, abundance, and rest. The *3* is associated with Venus, love, harmony, balance, intelligence, and the color yellow.

When *3* is found in the numeroscope, it indicates the possibilities of growth, relationship, understanding, equilibrium, ease, and peace. In esoteric psychology, the *3* signifies Mercury and the intellectual elements of adequate adaptation. In identity development, the *3* signifies the *initiative versus guilt crisis* from which arises the power of *purpose*.

Personality traits and behaviors associated with *3* include: animation, artistic, artistry, arts, beauty, brilliant, charm, communication, conceit, conversation, cooperation, creativity, cultivation, ease, energetic, enthusiasm, entertainment, envy, equilibrium, expansive, expression, extravagance, flirtatiousness, friendship, frivolous, good luck, grace, greed, growth, happiness, harmony, humor, indecision, imagination, inspiration, intelligence, joy, laziness, love, lucky, luxury, optimism, outspoken, peace, pleasure, poetry, popularity, relationships, romance, rhythms, self-expression, sociability, sociable, spirituality, superficiality, triviality, understanding, vanity, versatile, vision, wasteful, witty, words, and writing.

Number 4

Construction, Creation

The number *4* is the *tetrad*. It is represented by a solid and is the first feminine square. The *4* represents justice, is steadfast, and a perfect square. It is also the number of the elements, the seasons, the ages of man, lunar phases, and virtues. It represents the power to manifest ideas in the material world. It is said to be the *root of all manifested things*. In many ancient cultures the *4* symbolized the world, the Earth, and any Establishment. It is the number of foundations, solid matter, the points of the compass, the seasons, the (classical Greek) elements, the winds, completion, solidarity, stability, equilibrium, the (classical Greek) four kingdoms of matter. The *4* is action, activity, energy, power, strength, crisis, sacrifice, the square, the cross, and processes of building and creating solid, concrete forms in the material world. It is the four psychological functions in Analytic Psychology (Jungian). The *4* is associated with Saturn and/or Mars, the Earth, and the colors red, green, or brown.

Wherever the *4* is found in the numeroscope, it indicates the presence of activity and strong energies needed to overcome obstacles, conflicts, and crises. The power to manifest one's dreams in the material world and/or to actualize important relationships is present. In esoteric psychology, the *4* signifies Venus and the social elements of the ability to band together. In identity development, the *4* signifies the *competence versus inferiority crisis* from which arises the power of *competenc*e.

Personality traits and behaviors associated with 4 include: achievement, action, activity, aloofness, application, bitterness, building, calm, creativity, crises, energy, concentration, conflicts, conservation, construction, dedication, dejection, dependability, depth, determination, discipline, dull, economy, efficient, enduring, follow-through, form, foundation, fundamentals, gloomy, goal-orientation, growth, hardness, hard-working, ill health, impersonality, individuality, industrious, industry, joyless, limitation, management, melancholy, monotony, narrowness, organization, painstaking effort, patience, perseverance, planning, power, practical, practicality, repressive, respectable, restlessness, restriction, self-discipline, skill, stable, steady, strength, and struggles, and suspicious.

Number 5

Intelligence, Originality

The number *5* is called the *pentad* and represents man or humanity, especially in regards to creativity, intelligence, talents, and self-expression, i.e., especially those qualities that are most uniquely human and separate man from the rest of the animal kingdom. Thus, the *5* represents the Quintessence, humanity, the magician, magic, the (Western) senses, and the (Chinese) elements. The *5* is the masculine marriage number, because it unites the first female number and the first male number by addition. It has the virtue of being incorruptible, because all multiples of *5* end in *5*. The *5* is associated with Mars and/or Uranus, the Air, and the color blue.

Wherever the *5* is found in the numeroscope, it indicates the presence of intelligence, creativity, special talents, uniqueness, individual expression and possibly genius. In esoteric psychology, the *5* signifies Mars and the aggressive elements of the ability to defend and secure. In identity development, the *5* signifies the *identity versus role confusion crisis* from which arises the power of *fidelity*.

Personality traits and behaviors associated with 5 include: activity, adaptability, adventure, adventurous, belligerence, change, changeableness, clever, conceited, courage, creativity, criticalness, curiosity, discard, enterprise, expansiveness, experience, flexibility, freedom, haste, impulsiveness, individuality, intelligence, intuition, invention, irresponsibility, lustful, magnetism, movement, nervous, progress, promotion, resilient, restlessness, resourcefulness, sarcastic, scattering, sensuality, sexual, strife, temperament, thoughtlessness, uniqueness, unpredictability, unstable, variety, versatility, and vitality.

Number 6

Responsibility, Success

The number *6* is represented by the *hexad*. The *6* is the feminine marriage number, because it unifies *2* and *3* through multiplication. It is also considered the first perfect number and is the area of a *3-4-5* triangle. The *6* represents the benefits that come from activity and productivity. To the Pythagoreans, *6* was the perfect number since, when multiplied by itself it results in the number itself ($6 \times 6 = 42 \sim 4 + 2 = 6$). The *6* was also considered to be a perfect number because $\sim 1 + 2 + 3 = 6$. The *6* combines the ease, harmony, good luck, synthesis of the *3* with the polarity and awareness of the number *2*. The *6* is an active, productive, and successful number *3*. It brings good fortune, but through effort, productivity, and activity. The *6* is also related to the human soul, harmony, creation, love, marriage, domestic happiness, and matters of the heart, by some numerologists. The *6* is associated with Jupiter, the Earth element, productivity, and the color indigo.

Wherever the *6* is found in the numeroscope, it indicates a high likelihood of success and prosperity through work efforts. In esoteric psychology, the *6* signifies Jupiter and the religious elements of faith in leadership and tolerance. In identity development, the *6* signifies the *intimacy versus isolation crisis* from which arises the power of *love*.

Personality traits and behaviors associated with 6 include: beauty, burdens, carelessness, comfort, complacent, conscientiousness, conservative attitudes, creative, domesticated, domesticity, educational, legal, religious, and/or spiritual interests, exaggeration, expansion, family, friendliness, gossipy, harmonious, harmony, healing, honest, hypocrisy, idealistic, interfering, joyfulness, justice, loyal, luck, meddling, morale, morality, optimism, over-concern for others, over-expansiveness, overindulgence, parental, passion, productivity, prosperity, protection, reliability, responsibility, selfish, self-righteousness, service, social and artistic balance, trivial, trust, understanding, and wisdom.

Number 7

Thought/Consciousness

To the Pythagoreans the number *7* is represented by the *heptad* and is associated with the Greek maiden goddess Athene. They considered *7* to be a virgin number because it has no products, and a circle can never be broken into *7* equal parts. The *7* symbolizes the cosmic process of creativity. It combines the divine trinity of the *3* and the power of physical manifestation of the *4*. The *7* represents the stages of manifestation and the seven aspects of God as manifested through the seven stars or angels. It represents creation, divinity, and religious and fated activities. It symbolizes occult mysteries, magical ceremonies, and psychic and clairvoyant powers. The *7* is considered to be a difficult number to interpret in a specific and accurate manner. The *7* is associated with Saturn, religion, devotion, authority, royalty, the Earth element, and the color purple.

Wherever the *7* is found in the numeroscope, it is very likely that religion and spirituality figure prominently. Either the exoteric and/or the esoteric aspects of religion may be present. Strange and fated occurrences are likely as well. In esoteric psychology, the *7* signifies Saturn and the safety elements, and the abilities to escape from enemies and provide security. In identity development, the *7* signifies the *generativity versus stagnation crisis* from which arises the power of *caring*.

Personality traits and behaviors associated with 7 include: aloneness, aloof, analysis, authority, bureaucracy, calculation, confused, conservative attitudes, contemplative, depressive, dreamy, efficiency, escapism, exactitude, example, faith, fear, fussiness, impractical, intellectual snobbery, intelligence, introspection, intuition, investigation, knowledge, lazy, legal, religious, and/or spiritual interests, loneliness, malice, melancholy, metaphysics, moody, mystery, mystical, nagging, nervousness, perception, perfection, perfectionism, pessimism, philosophy, pride, psychology, religious or spiritual development, realities, reason, research, responsibility, science, secrecy, self-knowledge, self-righteousness, skepticism, silence, solitude, suspicion, thought, understanding, the unseen, verbosity, vision, and wisdom.

Number 8

Power/Sacrifice

The *8* is referred to as the *octad* or *ogdoad*. It is the first cube: *2* x *2* x *2* = *8*. Because it is the *4* (action, activity, energy, and crisis), divided by the *2* (externalization, separation, tension, and conflict), the *8* symbolizes the point of maximum dynamic activity, the point of the greatest energy and power. It is considered to symbolize material success and worldly involvement. The *8* is associated with the Sun and Uranus, activity, frustrations, busy work, and the colors rose and the transitional color between red and violet.

Wherever the *8* is found in the numeroscope, it indicates intense energy needed to finalize the details of and structure. At times the *8* can be very frustrating. At other times, it may feel exhilarating when our consciousness flows with the work we are performing. In esoteric psychology, the *8* signifies Uranus and the individualistic elements, and the abilities to depart from the past and develop better ways. In identity development, the *8* signifies the *integrity versus despair crisis* from which arises the power of *wisdom*.

Personality traits and behaviors associated with the 8 include: administration, authority, broad, business, busy work, capability, carelessness, comprehension, concentrated effort, control, cruelty, eccentric, efficiency, energy, extravagance, executive ability, extreme individualism, frustration, greed, guilt-ridden, haughty, hard work, impatience, lack, improvidence, leadership, loss, management, material accomplishment, materialism, money, obstinate, organization, power, promotion, rewards, ruthless, self-reliance, skill, strain, strength, struggle, success, tenacity, thoroughness, tough, unscrupulous, vindictiveness, and waste.

Number 9

Completion

The number *9* is referred to as the *nonad* or *ennead*. It is the first masculine cube. It is also considered incorruptible because no matter how many times it is multiplied, it reduces to itself. The *9* can be thought of as a very spiritual number or as a very lucky number because it is three *3*'s. The *9* is similar to the *7* in that it is a very spiritual number and one that prefers isolation and withdrawal. It is actually the last number in regards to numerology because all other numbers can be reduced to *1*, *2*, *3*, *4*, *5*, *6*, *7*, *8*, or *9*. The *9* represents the human gestation period, ending in the completion of one cycle and the beginning of the next. It is also similar to gestation in that the actual activity of creation is not visible to the material world. The *9* is may be associated with Uranus, Neptune, or Pluto. Because of its universal qualities, it may be associated with all the colors of the spectrum, bright blue, and psychedelic colors.

In the numeroscope, the *9* suggests creativity, spirituality, withdrawal, and completion. A *9* in the numeroscope indicates that the person will give birth, probably several times, to the development of spiritual ideas, mysticism, and psychic phenomena. In esoteric psychology, the *9* signifies Neptune and the utopian elements, and the yearning for better conditions.

Personality traits and behaviors associated with 9 include: attainment, benevolence, compassion, completion, creativity, dedication, devotion, disruption, emotion, expulsion, extremes, generosity, genius, imagination, impersonality, intellect, intensity, intuition, limitless power, meditation, mysticism, personal loss, philanthropy, psychic phenomena, regeneration, religious devotion, service, selflessness, shyness, ulterior motives, understanding of the spirit, upheaval, universal awareness, and universality.

Number 10

Rebirth

The number *10* is called the *decad*. It represents completion, infinity, and rebirth. It is also the number of our fingers and toes. The *10* is said to contain all the numbers because after *10*, the numbers repeat themselves. The number *10* is generally not used in numerology because the *10* is reduced to *1* in numerology (*1 + 0 = 1*). The *10* has characteristics of both the *0* and the *9*. In esoteric psychology, the 10 signifies Pluto and the universal welfare elements, and preservation through cooperation among individuals.

Number 0

Everything and Nothing

The *0* is not included in Pythagorean numerology. It represents *God unmanifest*, i.e., Spirit without Matter and without things. It is God before creation, especially physical or material creation. It is Divinity without awareness. The *0*, or circle is divine potential upon which no action has been taken. It is the cosmos before the cosmos comes into being, before the Big Bang, or whatever. It is also a symbol of infinity. The *0* also reminds us of the positive value of powerlessness. In metaphysical symbolism, a circle with a dot in its center indicates that creation or physical manifestation has begun. It especially symbolizes that the Spirit or God, has divided into individual parts so that it may come to know itself. This division is not real. It is the false perception of mater or material objects. In astrology, *God manifest* is represent by the symbol for the Sun. The Sun is the individualized spirit that sustains each of us. The *0* is not used in most numerological calculations or in the numeroscope. The reason is that *0* + any number = the number. The *0* has its own significance, but it does not add anything to numerological calculations.

Master Numbers

The term *master number* refers to two, three, or four numbers which are considered to be above and beyond the normal spectrum of the average human being. These numbers imply genius and superior accomplishments brought over from previous lives. Master numbers may possess greater potential or higher vibrations than other numbers. They may be highly charged and difficult to handle. They may take great effort to integrate into one's personality. Realizing the power of master numbers may require time and maturity. After interpreting a number as a master number, it is usually reduced numerically to a single digit, and the standard interpretation is applied as well.

The numbers *11*, *22*, *33*, and *44* have all been referred to as master numbers. Master numbers are interpreted before they are reduced to single digits. As previously mentioned, most numerologists recognized *11* and *22* as master numbers. A few use *33* as a master number, and even fewer use *44* as a master number. Some numerologists do not use any master numbers.

Number 11

Inspiration/Illumination

The number *11* refers to idealism and outstanding accomplishments that are largely intellectual or mental in nature. It often indicates artistic or musical talent. The individual with an *11* is said to be *inspired*, and he or she is usually an *inspiration* to others. An *11* may also display characteristics of a *2*. Of course, not everyone with an *11* is capable of manifesting the talents and characteristics of an *11*. In such cases, the *11* becomes an ordinary *2*.

Personality traits and behaviors associated with *11* include: altruism, aviation, creativity, confusion, debauchery, deception, delusion, destruction, dreamer, ecstasy, elation, electricity, escapism, evangelism, faith, fame, fanaticism, greatness, idealism, ideals, illumination, impracticality, independence, inner conflict, insight, inspiration, intangible, intuition, limelight, mysticism, nervousness, obligation, originality, peace, perversity, phobias, principles, psychic, radicalism, rebellious, religion, reverence, sacrifice, self-destruction, sensitivity, shyness, spirituality, spiritual vision, subconscious, tactlessness, truth, understanding, and uselessness.

Number 22

Masterful/Master Builder

The *22* is interpreted as a number of great material accomplishments, often through the use of spiritual or magical abilities. It is the most powerful of all the numbers. A person with a *22* turns dreams into reality. He or she is referred to as a Master Builder. A *22* may also display characteristics of a *4*. Of course, not every with a *22* is capable of manifesting the talents and characteristics of an *22*. In such cases, the *22* becomes an ordinary *4*.

Personality traits and behaviors associated with *22* include: achiever, ambition, broad vision, discipline, distribution, intense, limitless, materialistic, methodical, pressure, practicality, resourceful, self-confidence, strong, and success.

Number 33

Initiate/Master Teacher

The number *33* symbolizes the principle of guidance. It is the most influential of all numbers. The person with a *33* has made great spiritual accomplishments in previous lives. He or she has successfully integrated the *11* and the *22* and has risen to a higher level. He or she has become the Master Teacher, and his or her dharma or spiritual purpose is to uplift humanity spiritually by communicating the wisdom of the ages. He or she must forsake all personal ambitions.

The Master Teacher displays a high level of devotion to truth. He or she must seek understanding and wisdom before preaching to others. The Master Teacher must find original ways to encourage spiritual evolution. The arts, medicine, or some unconventional form of healing are possible mediums through which the Master Teacher addresses the public. He or she must share the truths he or she knows. If not, the Master Teacher may stagnate. His or her opportunities for further growth dwindle away until he or she performs the duties of the Master Teacher. A *33* may also display characteristics of a *6*. Of course, not every with a *33* is capable of manifesting the talents and characteristics of a *33*. In such cases, the *33* becomes an ordinary *6*.

Personality traits and behaviors associated with *33* include: artist, blessing, bravery, Christ-like, compassionate, courage, discipline, educator, guidance, healing, healer, honest, inspiration, love, martyr, monk, physician, protection, self-sacrifice, teacher of teachers, and truth.

The *33* manifests only when the birth day, the birth month, and the birth year (day/month/year) each add up to *11*, when the month and day add up to *22* and the year to *11*, when the month and year add up to *22* and the day to *11*, or the day and year add up to *22* and the month to *11*. For example, during the 21st century the years 2009, 2018, 2027, 2037, 2045, 2054, 2063, 2072, 2081, and 2090 add up to *11*. During the 20th century, only the year 1901 adds up to an *11*. Years like 1991 add up to a *2*. 1991 = 1 + 9 + 9 + 1 = 20 (1 + 9 = 10, 10 + 9 = 19, 19 + 1 = 20, 2 + 0 = *2*).

The master numbers *11*, *22*, and *33* are said to represent a triangle called the Triangle of Enlightenment. In relation to the Triangle, the number *11* represents the vision, *22* combines vision with action, and *33* offers guidance to the world.

Number 44

Masterful/Master Manager

The *44* is the number of the Master Manager. The Master Manager is extremely rare. He or she is a conscious bridge between the physical plane and higher planes or realms. The Master Manager is capable of manifesting whatever he or she focuses on with desire. He or she is learning to be a creator. A *44* may also display characteristics of an *8*. Of course, not every with a *44* is capable of manifesting the talents and characteristics of a *44*. In such cases, the *44* becomes an ordinary *8*.

Your Birthpath
The Key to Your Destiny
Chapter 3

I guide you in the way of wisdom and
lead you along straight paths.
Proverbs 4:11

You will make known to me the path of life;
In Your presence is fullness of joy;
In Your right hand there are pleasures forever.
Psalm 16:11

The *Birthpath Number* is the sum of the birth date. That is, it is the sum of the numbers in your month, day, and year of your birth expressed as a single digit or master number. The Birthpath Number is also referred to as the *Birth Path Number*, the *Date of Birth Number*, the *Life Path Number*, the *Destiny Number*, and the *Birth Force Number*. Unlike many of the numbers that make up the complete life plan, the Birthpath Number never changes.

The Birthpath—The Key To Destiny

The Birthpath signifies the traits with which one is born and which will continue the individual throughout life. It describes the person's life journey. The Birthpath reveals the direction or purpose of one's life. It shows the best way for one to fulfill his or her obligations in this life and the most harmonious manner to move through this lifetime. The Birthpath Number is like a seed planted on the day of birth. It refers to the greatest assets available in this life. Conscious awareness of the Birthpath number can bring clarity to what seemed to be chaotic. Knowledge of one's Birthpath Number can be used as a guide to actualizing one's full potential.

The wisdom that one has accumulated over the ages is carried by the Birthpath Number. It is part of the soul's spiritual, mental, and emotional heritage. However, everything that one has attained is not necessarily expressed by the Birthpath. The Birthpath Number expresses only those abilities, talents, and assets chosen by the soul for use in this particular lifetime. The talents and abilities acquired in past lifetimes are innate or present at birth. The Birthpath Number describes what has already attained.

Even though these qualities have already been acquired, the individual must pass through certain events, experiences, and challenges in order to discover them once again. Permission to follow the Birthpath as a child gives one a definite advantage in life and builds confidence and self-esteem.

Do not wrongly conclude that because one's Birthpath Number is greater than someone else's that he or she is are more spiritually advanced. That is a Birthpath of *8* is not greater than a *5* or a *2*. That is not how numerology works. (This true for all the numbers in the numeroscope.) Besides, playing the *"Holier Than Thou"* game is guaranteed to set one back in the game of spiritual growth and enlightenment if there were such a game.

The Birthpath Number is especially useful in determining vocational tendencies and possibilities. It describes the abilities, talents, and personality characteristics that will be needed to fulfill one's destiny, especially one's vocational destiny. However, even though we are born with one particular Birth path Number, it is possible to develop a new one during any particular life.

How to Find the Birthpath Number

The Birthpath Number is derived from the date of birth. First, reduce each unit (month/day/year) of the birth date to a single-digit or a master number (11, 22). Then add the three resulting digits or master numbers together.

Next, reduce this sum to a single digit or master number. In other words, convert the month to a single digit or master number. Then convert the day of birth to a single digit or master number. Next, add the total digits of year together and reduce this sum to a single digit or master number. Then add the individual digits representing the month, day, and year together.

Example #1

For example, if a person was born on October 3, 1975 (10/03/1975), add the digits of the month together -10. $1 + 0 = 1$. Add the digits of the day together -03. $0 + 3 = 3$. Add the digits of the year together -1975. $1 + 9 + 7 + 5 = 22$. Finally, add the month, day, and year digits together -1, 3, 22. $1 + 3 + 22 = 26$. Reduce 26. $2 + 6 = 8$. The Birthpath number for October 3, 1975 is *8*.

October 3, 1975
Birth Month: October (the 10th month)
Birth Day: 3
Birth Year: 1975
Birth Month: $10 = 1 + 0 = 1$
Birth Day: 3
Birth Year: $1975 = 1 + 9 + 7 + 5 = 22$
Add Month + Day + year: $1 + 3 + 22 = 26$
Reduce 26: $2 + 6 = 8$
The Birthpath Number is *8*. (Written as *8-Birthpath*)

October 10, 1975									
Month	October	10	=	$1 + 0$	=	1			
Day	3	3	=		=	3			
Year	1975	1975	=	$1 + 9 + 7 + 5$	=	22			
Total						26	=	$2 + 6$	=	8

Example #2

For example, if a person was born on November 26, 1973 (11/26/1973), add the digits of the month together -11. $1 + 1 = 2$. Add the digits of the day together -26. $2 + 6 = 8$. Add the digits of the year together -1973. $1 + 9 + 7 + 3 = 20$. Finally, add the month, day, and year digits together - 2, 8, 2. $2 + 8 + 2 = 12$. Reduce 12. $1 + 2 = 3$. The Birthpath number for November 26, 1973 is *3*.

November 26, 1973
Birth Month: November (the 11th month) = 11 = $1 + 1 = 2$
Birth Day: $26 = 2 + 6 = 8$
Birth Year: $1973 = 1 + 9 + 7 + 3 = 20$; $2 + 0 = 2$
Birth Month + Birth Day + Birth Year = $2 + 8 + 2 = 12$
Reduce 21: $2 + 1 = 3$
The Birthpath Number is *3*. (Written as *3-Birthpath*)

November 26, 1973										
Month	November	11	=	$1 + 1$	=			2		
Day	26	26	=	$2 + 6$	=			8		
Year	1973	1973	=	$1 + 9 + 7 + 3$	=	20	=	2		
Total								12	$1 + 2$	=	3

Example #3

For example, if a person was born on May 30, 1965 (05/30/1965), There is no need to add the digits of the month since it is a single digit—5. Add the digits of the day together -30. $3 + 0 = 3$. Add the digits of the year together -1965. $1 + 9 + 6 + 5 = 21$, and reduce = $2 + 1 = 3$. Finally, add the month, day, and year digits together -5, 3, 3. $5 + 3 + 3 = 11$. Since 11 is a master number, do not reduce it any farther. The Birthpath number for May 30, 1965 is *11*.

May 30, 1965
Birth Month: May (the 5th month) = 5
Birth Day: $30 = 3 + 0 = 3$
Birth Year: $1965 = 1 + 9 + 6 + 5 = 21$; $2 + 1 = 3$
Birth Month + Birth Day + Birth Year = $5 + 3 + 3 = 11$
The Birthpath Number is *11*. (Written as *11-Birthpath*)

May 30, 1965										
Month	May	5	=	5	=					5
Day	30	30	=	3 + 0	=					3
Year	1965	1965	=	1 + 9 + 6 + 5	=	21	=	2 + 1	=	3
Total										11

Interpreting the Birthpath Number

Birthpath 1

Individuality/Independence

Fulfilling your destiny in this lifetime will depend on you developing independence, self-sufficiency, and a strong sense of individuality. Your courage and convictions are being tested. You will be presented with obstacles and opportunities designed to bring out your personal creativity, your originality, and your self-reliance. In some way you need to be a pioneer who can set him- or herself apart from the crowd. Your will power is strong, and your vision of yourself and your world is unusual and unique. Some individuals with a birthpath of *1* are very creative and inventive and need opportunities to test out your ideas and theories. Their originality can be expressed through inventions that benefit society or through writing prose, fiction, poetry, or song lyrics. Some *1*'s are charismatic, dominant, and ambitious. They display executive ability and do well as leaders or managers. Some start their own businesses. Other *1*'s are rugged individualists who prefer to work alone and do best as private consultants. All *1*'s need to avoid becoming bossy, smug, or stubborn, on the one hand, and shy, meek, and lonely, on the other.

Possible careers for *1-Birthpaths* include any creative work, designer, engineer, entertainer, explorer, inventor, leadership positions, politics, show business, sports, and small business owner.

Birthpath 2

Cooperation/Support

Fulfilling your destiny in this lifetime will depend on you learning to work closely with others. It is important that you learn to interact easily with others, to understand their behavior and their underlying motivations. Harmony, diplomacy, cooperation, patience, and adjustment will enhance your chances of success. Developing sensitivity and empathy will also be helpful. Your success will depend either on sublimating your ego needs and assisting others or on allowing others to assist you. Pettiness or self-pity will diminish your ability to fulfill your destiny. There may be one particular person with whom you work well, who supports your goals, or whom you can help and support. It is possible that you will find a true soul mate during this lifetime. There may also be people who really try your patience and your sanity. You will need to balance relationship needs and goals with healthy self-esteem and setting appropriate limits.

Possible careers for *2-Birthpaths* include agent, attendant, clerk, counselor, diplomat, executive assistant, nurse, sales clerk, salesman, silent partner, small-business owner, teacher, technician, and trainer.

Birthpath 3

Self-Expression/Harmony

Fulfilling your destiny in this lifetime will depend on you learning to express yourself creatively. You will need to find an artistic form of self-expression that suits your temperament. You could be quite intuitive, imaginative, and artistic. You are talented and have a good sense of fashion or beauty. It is quite likely that you are a very sociable person who enjoys life and who prefers to avoid being overly structured. You are enthusiastic, optimistic, gregarious, and playful. Your pleasant personality contributes to your success. You may have a gift for writing, speaking, or acting. You may be prone to exaggerate and have a craving for change. Routine, discipline, and responsibility may bore you. You may fear criticism, rejection, and being controlled. You should blend your positive attitude with realism and common sense.

Possible careers for *3-Birthpaths* include artist, decorators, designer, disc jockey, grant writer, journalist, musician, party planners, poet, promoter, small business owner, and writer.

Birthpath 4

Accomplishment/Organization

Fulfilling your destiny in this lifetime will depend upon you developing a practical, constructive, and responsible approach to work. Your success will be enhanced by dependability, concentration, and precision. Your mind is logical, and your approach to work is traditional, conservative, and economic. You are organized and down-to-earth, and you pay attention to important details. You may learn one or more vocational or technical skills. Building something that is useful and of lasting value satisfies your need to be productive. You are not impressed by what is temporary, wasteful, or superficial. You will find that you work well when order is present and projects are challenging. However, too much chaos may undermine your efforts and efficiency. Some *4*'s do well as administrators. Your acceptance of responsibility and your need to do your best will attract permanent success. You need to be careful that you do not limit what you can accomplish due to being overly practical and conservative. Welcome a certain degree of change and novelty and avoid becoming too rigid and inflexible.

Possible careers for *4-Birthpaths* include accountant, administrator, attorney, board member, builder, businessman, chemist, CEO, construction, developer, executive, farmer, manager, real estate, and team player.

Birthpath 5

Creativity/Freedom

Fulfilling your destiny in this lifetime will depend on taking chances, searching for new opportunities, and trying out new and progressive ideas and developments. Your success is enhanced by your curiosity, versatility, boldness, and daring. You need to welcome change, variety, and uncertainty. You are enthusiastic about new ideas, places, and people. You are quick to adapt to the new and unexpected. Remember that the only thing that is permanent is change. You should follow unusual paths and investigate what is novel and cutting-edge. Yours is the path less taken. Personal freedom is important to you. In order to feel satisfied in your work and career, you need to feel that you are free to follow your own instincts. To get what you want, you may need to learn to sell yourself and your ideas. Following your heart may require that you become persuasive and influential in certain circles. You have a healthy respect for your abilities and contributions and, therefore, may feel that to do your best work you need to be left on your own. You may also feel that you deserve to have your needs and desires met. Indeed you do, but be careful not to become overly self-indulgent. Your mind is quick and intuitive. Your thinking is both deep and broad. You can be quite original and inventive. You are ahead of your time, capable of grasping new ideas and of seeing significant connections that others have missed. The down side here is that it is easy for you to feel bored, restless, and distracted. You may need to pursue more than one line of work at a time in order to be happy.

Possible careers for *5-Birthpaths* include communications, inventor, linguist, literary work, media, pubic figure, research, and travel.

Birthpath 6

Productivity/Service

Fulfilling your destiny in this lifetime will depend on your sense of responsibility for the welfare of others as well as on the services you can provide them. Your success is enhanced by cultivating your ability to adjust to the needs and demands of others. You may need to learn how to adjust and harmonize your own life with others, both personally and professionally. You may be a warm, nurturing individual who is concerned about family, friends, and community. You can be successful in endeavors related to home and family. Your own fulfillment comes from emphasizing the warmth and love of domestic traditions. You may take a position as a service provider or caregiver. You take on the role of a responsible caregiver, both professionally and personally. You fulfill your destiny when you provide help and support to others on an individual basis. However, it is possible that you will work with people in groups. Your understanding and compassion shows either way. Good career choices for you include catering, childcare, education, nursing, personal assistant, and teaching. For those who prefer work that involves less personal contact, you may be more satisfied with careers in the arts, entertainment, or decorative design. Some will do well designing useful products or operating a small business. You understand common human weaknesses, including your own your shortcomings. Be an anchor of dependability, but do not allow yourself to be a doormat or martyr. You will fulfill your destiny more effectively if you deal with and resolve any feelings of guilt and anxiety.

Possible careers for *6-Birthpaths* include caterer to small businesses, educator, home-maker, marriage counselor, medicine, minister, nursing, personal assistant, social work, veterinarian, and welfare worker.

Birthpath 7

Intensification/Specialization

Fulfilling your destiny in this lifetime will depend on your ability to develop your mind in the search of wisdom and truth. Your success will be enhanced by pursuing a scientific education and specializing in a particular field. You are able to analyze detailed facts and information and intuit the underlying connections among seemingly unrelated facts, events, and situations. You may find that it is necessary to spend a great deal of time alone in your pursuit of your career goals. Training your intuition to tap into deep levels of understanding will require that you take yourself out of the struggles for material needs and the fulfillment of social demands. Some may approach their destiny by living a lifestyle of study, solitude, and reflection, sanctioned by some traditional scientific, religious, or spiritual institution. Others may choose the life of a recluse or hermit. Most will satisfy their need for alone time by taking brief excursions into naturalistic settings, by spending time at a religious retreats, or by practicing meditation daily. No matter what method you use to accomplish your goals, it is important that you return to the social environment. You should test your conclusions by putting them into practice in the material and social realms. There will always be novel situations and new facts that require you to modify and, thus, expand and perfect your search for universal truths. It is also important that you share your discoveries, insights, and philosophies. You should teach what you have learned or pass it on in some form or manner.

Possible careers for *7-Birthpaths* include analytical work, archaeologist, astrologer, philosopher, research, self-employment in small business, and student.

Birthpath 8

Power/Financial Success

Fulfilling your destiny in this lifetime will depend on having the necessary drive to achieve the high goals you have set for yourself. Be sure that you have the incredible physical stamina needed to accomplish your tremendous ambitions. Thinking big works for you. You are hard-working, organized, decisive, and ambitious. You have executive ability and good financial sense, and you are quick to take advantage of every opportunity. You may be money-oriented, practical, and efficient. You are able to make a success out of whatever you undertake. You may crave power, control, and authority. It is likely that you will have opportunities to take charge of an organization and demonstrate your leadership skills. You may even manage large corporations. You are driven to be a material success and may be obsessed with over-the-top financial results. You may appear to be ruthless by the people you pass by on your way to the top.

Possible careers for *8-Birthpaths* include business banker, broker, executive, business franchise, CEO, financier, lawyer, manager, organizer, professional fields, and supervisor.

Birthpath 9

Humanitarian/Universalist

Fulfilling your destiny in this lifetime will depend on your ability to dream big and follow that dream. You are inspired to make to world a better place. You may direct your energy into producing much needed products and services, but you could also fulfill your destiny through volunteer work or community service. If other indications are present, you could become a community leader on a path towards increasing recognition and responsibility. Your success will be enhanced by developing a broadminded approach to life and by using your intuition to see the big picture. You do need to be careful that you do not overlook important details. In your search for truth, you will encounter ideas and concepts that reveal commonalities and draw people together. You are a humanitarian who understands and tolerates differences among people. You empathize with others and with the overall human condition. However, you may need to learn how to express your feelings of sympathy and generosity in ways that are more recognizable to others. Be sure that you actively pursue your dreams. It can be easy to depend on others financially and drift from dream to dream without ever accomplishing much of anything. Some possible career paths include community leader, ministry, or union leader.

Possible careers for *9-Birthpaths* include community leader, diplomat, doctor, lecturer, organizer, politician, statesman, and teacher.

Birthpath 11

Genius/Intuition

Fulfilling your destiny in this lifetime will depend on following the inspiration you are given. You are idealistic, intuitive, talented, intelligent, and artistic. You may be some kind of child prodigy with a special talent in music, mathematics, or literature. Some *11*'s may find that they are athletically talented and be world-class swimmers or tennis champions. Your thoughts, ideas, and interests are likely to be quite unusual, and yet you are very willing to share them with anyone who will listen. Your actions are determined by your unique worldview, which others might describe as religious, spiritual, metaphysical, or mystical. You may be attracted to topics such as hypnosis, consciousness, or enlightenment. You have an opportunity to achieve something great during this lifetime. You are being challenged to develop a specific gift, talent, or skill that will serve and inspire others. If you meet this challenge, you will be well rewarded, especially in terms of fame and prestige. You need to trust your intuition and channel your ideas and inspirations into concrete, physical forms that can be enjoyed by others. Since *11* is a higher octave of *2*, your success may be dependent on working with a partner who either inspires your creativity or takes care of your material and financial needs so that you can concentrate on your special talent. If you don't strive for personal excellence in your particular field, your opportunities will vanish and your destiny will become that of a *2-Birthpath*.

Possible careers for *11-Birthpaths* include advisor, humanitarian, theorist, leader, metaphysician, public servant, and teacher.

Birthpath 22

Spiritual Architect/Master Builder

Fulfilling your destiny in this lifetime will depend on your willingness to identify with a collective or universal need and put forth the necessary effort to create a solution for the need. You are most likely to be constructive, responsible, and goal-oriented. You may be energetic, hard-working, and ambitious. You want to make a difference in the world. Your success is enhanced by blending the inspirational and idealistic with the practical and profitable. You are respectful and demand respect. Ethics and justice are important to you, but you may need to work on service and cooperation. You are usually optimistic and patient, but you experience short bouts of depression when your expectations are not met. You may be quick to see solutions to complex problems. You will have opportunities to accomplish great things, especially in the arenas of politics, arts, humanities, industry, or business. Thinking big works for you. You can be most successful when you take charge of large-scale operations. Your actions may have global or universal effects. If you fail to aim high and work towards serving humanity, your opportunities will narrow and your destiny will become that of *4-Birthpath*.

Possible careers for *22-Birthpaths* include advisor, ambassador, CEO, global conglomerate, government representative, and mediator.

Birthpath 33

Guru/Initiate

Fulfilling your destiny in this lifetime requires that you surrender your personal will to that of the Self. You need to let go of your personal desires, ambitions, and possessions. You should seek spiritual truth, and you develop the ability to connect with your highest spiritual guidance instantly. You are building a conscious bridge connecting with higher realms of existence. This master number requires hours of daily devotion, discipline, and self-sacrifice. You are a teacher of teachers. Compassion, empathy, honesty, courage, inspiration, and intuition are your gifts to be shared freely. You are meant to teach the wisdom of the ages and to use your abilities for the spiritual uplifting of humanity. *33-Brithpaths* are extremely rare. Some individuals with *33-Birthpaths* manifest lesser degrees of the master number. If you fail to actualize any of this master number Birthpath, your destiny will become that of an enlightened and compassionate *6-Birthpath*.

Possible careers for *33-Birthpaths* include spiritual leader, guru, guide, healer, physician, monk, teacher, and martyr.

Universal Years, Months, and Days
Today is Tomorrow Yesterday
Chapter 4

A day may sink or save a realm.
Alfred, Lord Tennyson

Brave Helios, wake up your steeds
Bring the warmth the countryside needs
Peter Knight and Redwave

You can become blind by seeing each day as a similar one.
Each day is a different one, each day brings a miracle of its own.
It's just a matter of paying attention to this miracle.
Paulo Coelho

The creator of the universe works in mysterious ways.
But he uses a base ten counting system and likes round numbers.
Scott Adams

Many cycles are used in the practice of astrology. Cycles of 7 years and 12 years are especially important in predictive astrology. In numerology we work with cycles of 9. Pythagorean numerology uses the *base-10*. Whenever we use numbers, we use a *base value* for the numbers. The simplest base value to use is the one that uses the number *1* to represent one thing or one group of things. The number *2* represents two things or two groups of things. The number *3* represents three things or groups, and so on. Makes sense?

Yes, but the only reason it makes sense to us is because it is the customary base system that most of us learned as children. There is archaeological evidence that humans have been using the base-10 as far back as 37,000 years ago. When using base-10, we use single digits for the numbers zero through nine. We do not use a single-digit numeral for *10*. We write *10*, which stands for *1* ten and *0* ones. The number ten uses two digits. We have no single digit that stands for ten. Knowledge of bases other than base-10 is much more important today because computers use base-2and base-16 (hexadecimal).

Cycles of Nine

But why mention bases at all? Because when we apply numerology to a base-10 (decimal) system, we are automatically working with cycles of nine. If we were using base-2, we would be working with cycles of one. If we were working with base-16, we would be dealing with cycles of fifteen. Cycles of nine are the natural cycles in Pythagorean numerology. That doesn't mean that there are no cycles of ten, or cycles of eight. It means that the most natural cycle is a cycle of nine.

The American economist Edward Dewey (1895-1978), the founder of the Cycles Research Institute for the Interdisciplinary Study of Cycles, gathered and analyzed data regarding astronomical, geological, biological, agricultural, economic, social, and global cycles. Dewey found 26 documented nine-year-cycles, ranging from lynx abundance and venereal disease to cotton prices, capital exports, birth rates, marriage rates, death-rates, and church membership. He found a total of 212 documented cycles ranging between 8- and 9.9-years.

Each calendar year, month, and day has its own particular energy, meaning, or vibration which can be described or symbolized by a number. These numbers are referred to as the *Universal Year*, the *Universal Month*, and the *Universal Day*. They indicate what activities are favored by the particular year, month, and day.

The first two numbers of any year indicate characteristic energy, meaning, or vibration of that particular century. For 2010, the first two numbers are 20. Of course, they add up to 2 (2 + 0 = 2). The numerological value for the 21st century is *2*. The 21st century is one during which polarities integrate and opposites collide. Relationships are emphasized. Learning to cooperate and establishing harmony are major themes for this century.

The Universal Year

Any calendar year in general is called a *Universal Year*. The *Universal Year Number* is the numerological reduction of that particular year. The Universal Year Number describes the general trends and influences for that year. It forecasts the course of the world in general. The Universal Year Number indicates the universal vibration for the year and describes the collective environment active in everyone's lives. It describes the events and activities that are most likely to occur during the year.

In Pythagorean numerology the value of the Universal Year goes from *1* to *9*. Thus, there is a 9-year cycle in regards to the Universal Year. Universal Year cycles belong to everyone, or everyone belongs to the Universal Year cycles. Most numerologists employ the master numbers of *11* and *22* when calculating the value of the Universal Year. Using master numbers does not break up the 9-year cycle. A Universal Year cycle with a Universal Year of *11* goes from *1* to *11* (*2*), to *3*, to *4*, to *5*, to *6*, to *7*, to *8*, and to *9*. The Universal Year of *11* is interpreted as both an *11* and a *2*. A Universal Year cycle with a Universal Year of *22* goes from *1* to *2*, to *3*, to *22* (*4*), to *5*, to *6*, to *7*, to *8*, and to *9*. The Universal Year of *22* is interpreted as both a *22* and a *4*.

The universal year is determined by adding together each digit of the year and reducing the sum to a single digit or master number. For example, the numerological value of the current year, 2011, is: 2 + 0 + 1 + 1 = 4 The numerological value of 2010 is *4*.

Current Year	2011
Calculations	2 + 0 + 1 + 1
Numerological Meaning of 2011	4

The number of the last year 2009 is found by adding each digit of the year together—$2 + 0 + 0 + 9 = 11$. The numerological value of 2009 is *11*.

Current Year	2009
Calculations	$2 + 0 + 0 + 9$
Numerological Meaning of 2011	11

The numerological value of 1971 is: $1 + 9 + 7 + 1 = 18 = 1 + 8 = 9$. The numerological value of next year 1971 is *9*.

Current Year	1971
Calculations	$1 + 9 + 7 + 1$
Numerological Meaning of 2011	$18 = 1 + 8 = 9$

Meanings of the Universal Years

Universal Year 1

This year marks the beginning of a new nine-year cycle. It is a year of new beginnings. This is a year characterized by independence, individuality, initiative, novelty, self-reliance, spontaneity, and variety.

Universal Year 2

Relationships of all types are emphasized. It is characterized by adaptability, adjustability, coordination, cooperation, partnership, receptivity, harmony, and union. Competition, rivalry, and confrontation are also part of a *2-Uersonal-Year*. This year brings patient development.

Universal Year 3

This year emphasizes the productive use of skills and talents, the fulfillment of dreams and ambitions. Creativity, imagination, inspiration, and self-expression are highlighted. Successes, communications, and social life are prominent.

Universal Year 4

This year brings with it confrontations, crises, creative tensions, and the use of personal power. Very often there are a number of obstacles to be overcome in the process. A *4-Universal-Year* demands hard work, discipline, concentration, patience, intense drive, and, practical actions. This year is good for taking care of business and for putting down roots.

Universal Year 5

This year brings a variety of new opportunities, new people, and new situations. Flexibility is important. Spontaneity, enthusiasm, and restlessness are characteristic. This is a time for breaking free of the past.

Universal Year 6

This year is a time for enjoying an atmosphere of harmony, relationships, productivity, and success. This is a good time to be surrounded by friends, family, home, beauty, health, food, and everyday luxuries. Take care of others. Honor your responsibilities and obligations.

Universal Year 7

This is a good time to withdraw from the outer world and to focus on the meaning of your life as experienced during the past six years. It is a time for thoughtfulness, introspection, meditation, self-examination, and deliberation.

Universal Year 8

The challenges of living in the material world are emphasized. This year tests personal beliefs and philosophies in the real world. Taking charge is important.

Universal Year 9

Endings, completion, transformation, rebirth, and recycling are key themes this year. The concerns, affairs, and business of the past eight years—*certain* relationships, interpersonal situations, vocational matters, and emotional issues—will conclude. It is important to let this process complete itself without interference.

Universal Year 11

This year it is important to follow hunches, ideas, and intuition. Emotions are highly sensitized, and intellect is sharp. Be open to inspiration, visions, and revelations.

Universal Year 22

This year is potentially a year of self-actualization, self-mastery, and personal transformation. Opportunities to reach goals and actualize ideals are available.

The Universal Month

Each calendar month is called a *Universal Month*. Just as each year has a vibration, each month has its own energy, meaning, or vibration, also described or symbolized by a number. The *Universal Month Number* modifies the general trends and influences of the Universal Year during that particular month. The Universal Month Number should always be interpreted in relation to the Universal Year Number. In some ways it may strengthen or weaken the influence of the Universal Year Number. More precisely, it describes the stage of development of the Universal Year Number. Most numerologists employ the master numbers of *11* and *22* when calculating the value of the Universal Month Number.

The Universal Month Number is the sum of the digits of the month added to the Universal Year Number. For example, the Universal Month Number for January 2011 is the sum of January and the Universal Year Number for 2011: $1 + (2 + 0 + 1 + 1 = 4) = 5$. The Universal Month Number for January 2010 is *5*.

Current Month	January	1
Universal Year Number	2011	4
Calculations		$1 + 4$
Universal Year Number		5

The Universal Month Number for February 2012 is the sum of February and the Universal Year Number for 2010: $2 + (2 + 0 + 1 + 2 = 5) = 7$ The Universal Month Number for February 2012 is *7*.

Current Month	February	2
Universal Year Number	2012	5
Calculations		$2 + 5$
Universal Year Number		7

The Universal Month Number for March 1987 is the sum of March and the Universal Year number for 1987: $3 + (1 + 9 + 8 + 7 = 25 = 2 + 5 = 7) = 10 = 1 + 0 = 1$. The Universal Month Number for

March 1987 is *1*.

Current Month	March						3	
Universal Year Number	1987	1 + 9 + 8 + 7	=	25	2 + 5	=	7	
Calculations							10	1 + 0
Universal Year Number								1

Meanings of the Universal Months

Universal Month 1

This is the month for new beginnings—a perfect time to begin a new project, make a fresh start, or try on a new attitude.

Universal Month 2

This month emphasizes an increasing awareness of others, an interest in relationships of all kinds, and a time to take into account the needs, desires, and motivations of others. Partnerships, lovers and friends, competitors and enemies take on added significance.

Universal Month 3

This could be a very social month—dates, parties, social gatherings, and group activities. Relationships and shared pleasures are characteristic of this month. Friends, partners, lovers, spouses, and fiancés as well as more casual acquaintances are emphasized.

Universal Month 4

This is a month of actions, challenges, restrictions, and obstacles, and it requires concentration, discipline, organization, patience, perseverance, hard work, and attention to details. Some form of crisis may push past personal limitations. It is a month of creative tension and possible confrontations.

Universal Month 5

This month brings change, excitement, enthusiasm, novelty, spontaneity, and variety with a pinch of restlessness. There are new opportunities to investigate, new people to meet, and new freedoms to experience. Expect the unexpected. Flexibility is an important prerequisite to getting the most out of this month, much less make progress. The pace of this month is rapid and largely unencumbered.

Universal Month 6

This is a month of optimism, understanding, justice, and reciprocation if you take responsibilities and duties seriously. New opportunities may sprout from past accomplishments. Vocational and financial matters tend to go well, as do interpersonal relationships. This is a good month for domestic conditions, marriage, and weddings.

Universal Month 7

It is a month for thoughtfulness, introspection, meditation, self-examination, and deliberation. It is a time to analyze and reflect, to develop new insight and a new philosophy.

Universal Month 8

This month is one for acting on the thoughts, ideas, and philosophies. It is one of intense, dynamic activity. Broad comprehension and good judgment can lead to expanding business opportunities, making new investments, and signing favorable contracts. Enterprise and corporations are favored.

Universal Month 9

Endings, transformation, rebirth, and recycling are key themes this month. It is a month for subjective progress and growth and for the elimination of what is no longer useful. It is a good time for performing selfless service or promoting brotherhood and universal love.

Universal Month 11

This month emphasizes idealism, religion, mysticism, renunciation, and illumination. Intuition and psychic perception may be heightened during this month. On a material level, this month favors invention and technical genius.

Universal Month 22

This month is potentially a month of self-actualization, self-mastery, and personal transformation. Demonstrate a masterful capacity to combine materialism and idealism, inspiration and practicality. Turn abstract conceptions into practical visions. Projects undertaken during this month can bring about wide-scale improvements, possibly having regional, national, or even international consequences.

The Universal Day

Just as each year and each month has a vibration, each day has its own energy, meaning, or vibration, also described or symbolized by a number. Each calendar day is called a *Universal Day*. The *Universal Day Number* modifies the general trends and influences of the Universal Month Number for that particular day.

The Universal Day Number should always be interpreted in relation to the Universal Month Number. In some ways it may strengthen or weaken the influence of the Universal Month Number. More precisely, it describes the stage of development of the Universal Month Number. Most numerologists employ the master numbers of *11* and *22* when calculating the value of the Universal Day Number. Acting in concert with the energy of the day turns the Universal Day Number into a lucky one.

The *Universal Day Number* is the sum of the digits of the day added to the Universal Month Number. For example, the Universal Day Number for January 13, 2011 is the sum of 13 and the Universal Month Number for January 2011: $13 + 5 = (1 + 3 = 4) + 5 = 9$. The Universal Day Number for January 13, 2010 is *9*.

Current Day	January 13, 2011	13	=	1 + 3	=	4
Universal Month Number	January 2011	1 + 2 + 1 + 1	=	5		5
Calculations						9
Universal Day Number						9

The Universal Day Number for February 6, 2011 is the sum of 6 and the Universal Month Number for February 2011: $6 + 6 = 12 = 1 + 2 = 3$. The Universal Day Number for February 6, 2010 is *3*.

Current Month	February 6, 2011	6	=	6	5	
Universal Year Number	February 2011	2 + 2 + 1 + 1	=	6		
Calculations				12	=	1 + 2
Universal Year Number						3

Meanings of the Universal Days

Universal Day 1

Action. A day to promote your interests and accentuate your individuality. A day to be assertive, original, and spontaneous. Take a chance, welcome new opportunities, start something new.

Universal Day 2

Cooperation. A day that emphasizes significant relationships and increases your awareness of the needs and desires of others. This can be a favorable time for romance. Competition or confrontations are possible. Express yourself with tact and diplomacy. Balance assertion and individuality with patience and cooperation.

Universal Day 3

Expression. A pleasant day and a good time for self-expression, creativity, and communication. This day is a favorable time for socializing, entertaining, and enjoying the company of others. Today could bring joy, fulfillment, and happiness. Good for romance, taking chances, and financial gain.

Universal Day 4

Construction. Today emphasizes the practical and constructive sides of life. It is a day for building a solid foundation. A day that requires work, drive, organization, and scheduling. The use of energy or force to overcome an obstacle.

Universal Day 5

Creation. A change of pace and attitude. Transform any excessive, restless energy into creative insights, new ideas, mind expansion, travel, sports, or games. A time for changes, for the expression of personal freedom, for spontaneity, new opportunities, and going with the flow.

Universal Day 6

Production. A day to return to your responsibilities. This day can be a very productive one. Success comes from a combination of skillful effort and available resources. Family, home, community, health, service, food, and everyday luxuries are emphasized.

Universal Day 7

Perfection. Take time for yourself away from social engagements and most everyday activities. A day to withdraw, read a book, or meditate. This day stresses quietude, introspection, self-improvement, religious concerns, ideals, and spirituality.

Universal Day 8

Organization. Today is good for energetic activities, expressions of power, material accomplishments, and purposeful actions. Goals are reached; obstacles overcome. This day emphasizes finances, money, investments, business, enterprise, and corporations. Good judgment can lead to signing favorable contracts, making wise investments, and expanding business opportunities.

Universal Day 9

Selflessness. A good day to complete projects and similar endeavors. A day of endings, saying goodbye, and letting go. Possibly the ending of a relationship. Loss or sorrow. A time for performing selfless service or promoting brotherhood and universal love.

Universal Day 11

Inspiration. A day with great creative, religious, or spiritual potential. Today emphasizes idealism, intuition, and illumination. This day favors invention and technical genius on the material plane and psychic perception on the spiritual plane.

Universal Day 22

Internationalism. This is a day for actualizing your highest goals and ideals. A time for taking action in order to accomplish your plans. Demonstrate a masterful capacity to combine materialism and idealism successfully.

Your Personal Years, Months, and Days
Days of Future Passed
Chapter 5

What will this day be like? I wonder.
What will my future be? I wonder.
Richard Rodgers & Oscar Hammerstein II

This is the day the LORD has made;
let us rejoice and be glad in it.
Psalm 118:24

Man's days are determined; you have decreed
the number of his months and have set
limits he cannot exceed.
Job 14:5

The day which we fear as our last is but the birthday of eternity.
Seneca

Everyone is affected by the Universal Year, Universal Month, and Universal Day to some degree. Each of us is also influenced by our *Personal Year*, our *Personal Month*, and our *Personal Day*. The influences of the Personal Years, Months, and Days normally dominate the influences of the Universal Years, Months, and Days. When our Personal Years, Months, and Days are compatible with the Universal Years, Months, and Days, their influences are strengthened. When they are incompatible with the Universal Years, Months, and Days, their influences are weakened.

Your Personal Year

The Personal Year is one of several methods used in numerology for forecasting future trends and is probably one of numerology's most powerful predictive tools. Personal Years, like Universal Years, come in nine-year cycles. Each nine-year cycle has a beginning and an ending and seven years of development in between. Each year of any nine-year cycle has its own particular vibration. Each Personal Year offers opportunities to develop new skills and talents that are in harmony with the Personal Year's number. The Personal Year number indicates the numerological vibration for each year of the nine-year-cycle. The numerological vibration of the Personal Year describes the best way to approach that particular year. For example, if you are in a 1-Personal-Year, you are in a year of new beginnings, characterized by independence, individuality, initiative, novelty, self-reliance, spontaneity, and variety. You should focus is on yourself and your personal aspirations.

The Personal Year is simple to calculate and only a little more difficult to interpret. To determine the numerical vibration of any Personal Year, all you need is the day and month of birth and the current year. As with Universal Years, I use the master numbers *11* and *22* when interpreting Personal Years.

To calculate your Personal Year, add your birth day (not birthdate!) plus your birth month and the current calendar year (Universal Year). For example, let's assume you were born April 20, 1986 and the current year is 2010. Your birth day is 20, and your month is April, the 4th month of the year. Your birth month is simplified by adding the one or two digits—0 and 4—together. $0 + 4 = 4$. Your birth day is simplified by adding the one or two digits—2 and 0—together. $2 + 0 = 2$. Add the number of your birth day to the number of your birth month. $2 + 4 = 6$. Add the four digits of the current year—2010—together. $2 + 0 + 1 + 0 = 3$. Add the number of the current year to the sum of the birth day and the birth month: $6 + 3 = 9$.

Birthdate: April 20, 1986
Birth Month: April (the 4*th* month)
Birth Day: 20
Birth Year: 1986
Current Year: 2011
The Personal Year Number is *1* (written *1-Personal-Year*).

Birthdate – April 20, 1986/Current Year – 2011									
Birth Month	April	=	4	=	4				
Birth Day	20	=	2 + 0	=	2				
Current Year	2011	=	2 + 0 + 1 + 1	=	4				
Total					10				
Reduced Total					10	=	1 + 0	=	1

Let's do another.

Birthdate: May 13, 1994
Birth Month: May (the 5th month)
Birth Day: 13
Birth Year: 1986
Current Year: 2011
Birth Month: $0 + 5 = 5$
Birth Day: $1 + 3 = 4$
Current Year: $2 + 0 + 1 + 1 = 4$
Sum: $5 + 4 + 4 = 13 = 1 + 3 = 4$
The Personal Year Number is *4* (written *4-Personal-Year*).

Birthdate – May 13, 1994/Current Year - 2011									
Birth Month	May	=	5	=	5				
Birth Day	13	=	1 + 3	=	4				
Current Year	2011	=	2 + 0 + 1 + 1	=	4				
Total					13				
Reduced Total					13	=	1 + 3	=	4

Let's do one more.

Birthdate: October 25, 1963
Birth Month: October (the 10th month)
Birth Day: 25
Birth Year: 1963
Current Year: 2009
Birth Month: $1 + 0 = 1$
Birth Day: $2 + 5 = 7$
Current Year: $2 + 0 + 0 + 9 = 11$
Sum: $1 + 7 + 11 = 19 = 1 + 9 = 10 = 1 + 0 = 1$
The Personal Year number is *1* (written *1-Personal-Year*).

Birthdate – October 25, 1963/Current Year - 2009									
Birth Month	October	=	10	=	1 + 0	=	1		
Birth Day	25	=	25	=	2 + 5	=	7		
Current Year	2009	=	2009	=	2 + 0 + 0 + 9	=	11		
Total							19		
Reduced Total							19	=	1 + 9 = 10 = 1 + 0	=	4

Meanings of the Personal Year

Personal Year 1

This year marks the beginning of a new nine-year cycle. It is a year of new beginnings, a year characterized by independence, individuality, initiative, novelty, self-reliance, spontaneity, and variety. The focus is on you and your aspirations. You may use this year to develop new skills and talents, launch new projects, pursue your aspirations, and focus on self-development. Let your sense of selfhood (who you think you are) develop and expand as you face novel ideas and situations. Over these next twelve months you will be presented with what may seem to be an unending flow of new ideas, feelings, opportunities, and relationships.

Each new experience will give way to another. During the first six months, let the stream flow. Don't be too quick to hold on to any one idea or experience. During the last half of the year you will need to start making choices as to what you want to develop more fully. Don't be surprised if you find it difficult to stick to any one thing for very long. What you start this year will unfold over the following eight years. Choose wisely, though, because, in one way or another, the choices you make this year will serve as the foundation for the rest of this cycle. You may find this year to be one of increased vitality and subjectivity, strength and self-centeredness.

Some may display leadership skills and find themselves working with a degree of power and authority. In general, your health will be good, and you may feel more energized and lively than you have felt in a long time. Vocationally, you will do your best work when working along.

Interpersonally, some people may perceive you as being standoffish or conceited this year. This is the year to develop self-reliance, initiative, and a healthy sense of self-esteem. Healthy self-esteem will help you may avoid the feelings and traps of both inferiority and superiority, either of which could sabotage the purpose of this year.

Personal Year 2

You are entering the second year of your nine-year personal cycle. During this year your focus is on others, especially those people who are most important to you. Your awareness and understanding of others grow this year. Those others include both friends and lovers as well as competitors and enemies. This year emphasizes relationships of all types and is characterized by adaptability, adjustability, coordination, cooperation, partnership, receptivity, harmony, and union. Competition, rivalry, and confrontation are also part of a 2-Personal-Year. You will become more aware of how others may be helpful or hurtful. In order to get your needs met and your desires fulfilled, you will need to take into consideration the needs, desires, and motivations of others. If you fail to take the time to understand the inner workings of other people, you will find yourself on a path of loneliness and suspicion over the next seven years. This year emphasizes the development of tact, diplomacy, and patience as well as the ability to take a supportive role in the background. Domestic affairs and issues of giving and receiving may be prominent this year. Some may find themselves focusing on their home life and their parents, especially their mother. Some may deal with the public this year. Health-wise, your drive and vitality may not be as powerful as they were last year. Vocationally, you will do your best work when working with a partner or a team.

Interpersonally, this is a year for establishing long-term relationships, both romantically and otherwise. Financially, a 2-Personal-Year is a slow, conservative year, a time to limit spending while focusing on accumulating resources.

Personal Year 3

You are entering the third year of your nine-year personal cycle. This year your focus is on your own interests, needs, and desires. A 3-Personal-Year has the potential for bringing about fulfillment, happiness, and joy. This year emphasizes the productive use of your skills and talents and the fulfillment of your dreams and ambitions. Creativity, imagination, inspiration, and self-expression are highlighted this year. You may get involved with the arts, music, acting, or teaching. The 3-Personal-Year is about the joys of living, the pleasures of life, enjoyment, and entertainment. It is easy to be overly extravagant during this year so it is important to set some limits. The 3-Personal-Year is usually a year filled with social activity. You will find that your interests flow harmoniously with the people in your life. Relationships, shared pleasures, and affection are emphasized. Friends and companions abound. Your energies and interests blend harmoniously with those around you. This year can bring many brief flirtations as well as serious romances. There may be a tendency to go overboard, so it is important that you choose your associates and social affairs carefully. Vocationally, work and career go well, possible promotions as long as you pull yourself away from your social life to get your work done. The 3-Personal-Year is often an important financial year, a good time to accumulate money, property, and riches. Be sure to set reasonable limits on your spending.

Personal Year 4

You are entering the fourth year of your nine-year-personal-cycle. This year is often the most active and challenging year of the entire cycle. This year you will be required to give your ideas, dreams, and plans some form of concrete manifestation. You will be building a solid foundation that you will use during the next five years. Sometimes these foundations manifest as concerns involving home, family, real estate, property, or merchandise. This is a time to build a power base and consolidate your strength. This year brings with it confrontations, crises, creative tensions, and the use of personal power. Very often there are a number of obstacles to be overcome in the process. A 4-Personal-Year demands hard work, discipline, concentration, patience, intense drive, and, practical actions. Organization, attending to details, sustained effort, perseverance, and following a schedule or budget will be necessary in order to overcome restrictions, limitations and roadblocks. Your responsibilities will increase, and your skills and self-confidence will be tested. If you put forth the effort to handle the situations that come at you this year, you will be well rewarded vocationally and financially. However, you may be presented with relationship problems, possibly due to neglect. You will have to make good faith efforts in any relationship worth keeping. Also, keep your health in mind. Don't let working, or over-working, wear you out.

Personal Year 5

You are entering your 5-Personal-Year, the middle or midpoint of your nine-year personal cycle. Your 5-Personal-Year is a year of changes and a reprieve from some pressures and responsibilities. Your first four years were years of discovering, building, adding to yourself new traits, talents, and abilities as well as extending yourself into the material world in new ways. What you have developed over the last four year will now serve as the basis or foundation for expressing yourself in the world and sharing what you have with your friends, family, community, society, or culture.

The 5-Personal-Year brings a change of pace and attitude and represents a turning point in consciousness. This is the year of creative transformation and the expression of true individuality, a year for the expression of your creativity and unique talents. A 5-Personal-Year brings a variety of new opportunities, new people, and new situations. Flexibility is important. You may feel more spontaneous and enthusiastic, or even excessively restless. You desire the freedom to express yourself in new ways. A 5-Personal-Year can bring new ideas, mind expansion, traveling, and/or an interest in sports, games, or the great outdoors. The task for the 5-Personal-Year is to embrace the new without abandoning the foundations you established last year. This year can be favorable for career, finances, and relationships if you can integrate the new with the old.

Personal Year 6

You are entering your 6-Personal-Year. This is a year during which you can begin to concentrate on what you have at hand. During your 6-personal-year, you return to the structures you built and the issues you faced during your 4-Personal-Year—home, family, love, relationships, career—but minus struggling with the challenges and the confrontations of the 4-Personal-Year. During your 6-Personal-Year you will be able to enjoy the fruits of your labors and the foundations established two years early. The 6-Personal-Year is a time for enjoying an atmosphere of harmony, relationships, productivity, and success. You will tend to find yourself surrounded by the best in friends, family, home, beauty, health, food, and everyday luxuries. All the resources that you need will be available to you as long as you take your responsibilities and duties seriously. This is a year of optimism, understanding, justice, and reciprocation. The more you give the more you will receive. Your morale is high. While you will be making the most of whatever you have already accomplished, you will also be able to make the most of new opportunities. Vocational and financial matters tend to go well, as do your interpersonal relationships with friends, family, and co-workers. This is a good month for marriage and weddings in general.

Personal Year 7

You are entering your 7-Personal-Year. The number 7 symbolizes sacred cosmic processes and the number of all physical life. You may become unusually aware of your destiny, fate, and the cosmic processes at work in your life. The 7-Personal-Year may also bring with it the unpredictable and the irrational. You, or someone close to you, may feel compelled to act in certain ways. Social activities may take a back seat to intellectual and/or spiritual pursuits. The 7-Personal-Year is a year during which many people enter some degree of seclusion. This is a good time to withdraw from the outer world and to focus on the meaning of your life as experienced during the past six years. You should analyze and reflect on what you have learned about yourself and your world and develop new insight and a new philosophy based on your recent experiences. It is a time for thoughtfulness, introspection, meditation, self-examination, and deliberation. Your intuition may become usually active and sharp. Your thoughts turn towards self-improvement, idealism, perfectionism, and spirituality. Your intuition may become usually active and sharp. You could become interested in reading about and studying philosophy, religion, or metaphysics. You could even specialize in some form of esoteric studies. This is the year to discover your inner light, or, if the inner light is already a part of your life, to develop a deeper connection with it. You should find solutions and make important decisions this year.

Personal Year 8

You are entering your 8-Personal-Year. The pace of the 8-Personal-Year is a highly accelerated one. The challenges of living in the material world may occupy all your time and energy. This year you are required to test out your personal beliefs and philosophies in the material world. In addition to testing your beliefs this year, you will be reaping the results of your last 1-Personal-Yearpersonal-year. You will be required to further the ideas, plans, and activities that you began eight years ago. During the 1-Personal-Year you were free to try out new ideas and behaviors without much input from your environment. During your 8-Personal-Year you will meet both expected and unexpected challenges to your plans and activities. The 8-Personal-Year-year is often the most active, energetic, and dynamic year of the nine-year cycle. You will have abundant energy and determination to accomplish your goals this year. You may not have been aware of this great internal power until now. People, institutions, and other environmental obstacles will force you to tap into inner resources that you never knew you had. You will need to be organized and efficient. Planning, drive, detachment, and good judgment will be helpful. Potentially, this year offers opportunities for advancement, promotions, leadership, material accomplishment, and financial gain. Recognition and publicity are yours if you want them. Expect to broaden your comprehension and transcend previous limitations. This year is not particularly favorable for interpersonal relationships, so you will need to be especially sensitive and compassionate in those relationships that you value.

Personal Year 9

You are entering your 9-Personal-Year. This year is the final one of this nine-year cycle. Endings, completion, transformation, rebirth, and recycling are key themes this year. From the concerns, affairs, and business of the past eight years—certain relationships, interpersonal situations, vocational matters, and emotional issues—will conclude during this year. It is important that you let this process complete itself without interference. You will need to finish projects and goals of the cycle that is closing. Some friendships and associations will fall by the wayside. Let go of what has become useless and outgrown. Anxiety, fear, sadness, and other forms of resistance to change are natural reactions to the events of the 9-Personal-Year. Accept and honor whatever feelings you may be experiencing, but do your best to let go of whatever is leaving your life this year. Some losses will be gradual, others sudden. Allow yourself to grieve in your own way and at your own pace. There is no wrong way to grieve or say goodbye. It is vital to complete this process so that you will have room in your heart and life for the new blessings to come next year. The good to come during your 1-Personal-Year depends on your ability to let go and forgive. It is also important that you give thanks for and appreciate whatever is leaving your life during your 9-Personal-Year. Cultivating a universal outlook and grasping a sense of eternity will be helpful. By cultivating an attitude that fosters love, compassion, tolerance, detachment, and selflessness, you will be rewarded with increased love, wisdom, understanding, and insights. Before this year is finished, you may become aware to some degree of the nature and direction of your next nine-year cycle. Since each new cycle builds on the foundations provided by the previous cycles, it is highly unlikely that everyone and everything in your life will be lost. Much of your past will continue with you into your new 1-Personal-Year.

Personal Year 11

You are entering an 11-Personal-Year, which can be one of the two master years. This year it is important that you follow your hunches, your inspiration, and your intuition. Your emotions are highly sensitized, and your intellect is sharp. You can be unusually open to new ideas, visions, and revelations. This can be a year of consciousness expansion or possibly an increased interest in the arts. At the physical level, you can be creative and inventive. Work with science, computers, telephones, cell phones, aviation, space travel, electricity, radiation, and magnetism can be beneficial to you. On a more spiritual level, you can be capable of developing psychic abilities or spiritual healing. This can be a year of illumination and self-discovery. Idealism, religion, mysticism, and spirituality figure prominently. You could take up mediation and metaphysical studies. You may gain insights into spiritual evolution. Much is nebulous or intangible this year. It is important to stay as grounded as much as you can in order to gain the benefits of this year. For some, this year can lead to increased fame if there are other indications.

If you do not pursue the vibrations of the number *11* and make them a priority, the 11-Personal-Year becomes a 2-Personal-Year. If the *11* becomes a *2*, this year will bring an increasing awareness and understanding of other people. These others include both friends and lovers as well as competitors and enemies. This year emphasizes relationships of all types and is characterized by coordination, cooperation, partnership, harmony, and union. Competition, rivalry, and confrontation are also part of a 2-Personal-Year. You will become more aware of how others may be helpful or hurtful. In order to get your needs met and your desires fulfilled, you will need to take into consideration the needs, desires, and motivations of others. If you fail to take the time to understand the inner workings of other people, you will find yourself on a path of loneliness and suspicion over the next seven years. This year emphasizes the development of tact, diplomacy, and patience as well as the ability to take a supportive role in the background. Domestic affairs and issues of giving and receiving may be prominent this year. Your drive and vitality may not be as powerful as they were last year. Vocationally, you will do your best work when working with a partner or a team. Interpersonally, this is a year for establishing long-term relationships, both romantically and otherwise. Financially, a 2-Personal-Year is a slow, conservative year, a time to limit spending while focusing on accumulating resources.

Personal Year 22

You are entering a 22-Personal-Year, which can be one of the two master years. This year is potentially a year of self-actualization, self-mastery, and personal transformation. During a 22-Personal-Year you have opportunities to reach your highest goals and ideals. You can demonstrate a masterful capacity to combine materialism and idealism, inspiration and practicality. You may turn abstract conceptions into practical realizations. It is possible to achieve your goals and accomplish great things this year. The 22-Personal-Year is a year of destiny during which you have generous and abundant opportunities to work with your karmaphalas (the results of previous acts {karma}) both good/pleasant and bad/unpleasant. The secret for making the most of this year is to keep in mind that your actions should be performed while keeping the good of society or of all humanity in mind. You should view yourself as an agent of change and as someone who can make personal sacrifices from which the world will benefit. You may embody the ideals, needs, and concerns of specific groups or communities. Even so, you will probably have to act on your own. You may even experience yourself as independent and possibly alone. While it is unlikely that you can completely abandon the demands of the ego, you need to keep the universal good foremost in your thoughts.

If you use the energies of your 22-Personal-Year predominately for your personal gain, the *22* will convert to a *4*. As a 4-Personal-Year, this year will be a very active one with many challenges. This year you will be required to give your ideas, dreams, and plans some form of concrete manifestation. You will be building a solid foundation that you will use during the next five years. Sometimes these foundations manifest as concerns involving home, family, real estate, property, or merchandise. This is a time to build a power base and consolidate your strength. This year brings with it confrontations, crises, creative tensions, and the use of personal power.

Very often there are a number of obstacles to be overcome in the process. A 4-Personal-Year demands hard work, intense drive, and, practical actions. Organization, attending to details, and following a schedule or budget will be necessary in order to overcome limitations and roadblocks. Your responsibilities will increase, and your self-confidence will be tested. If you put forth the effort to handle the situations that come at you this year, you will be well rewarded vocationally and financially. You may be presented with relationship problems. You will have to make good faith efforts in any relationship worth keeping.

Personal Months and Personal Days

In addition to Personal Years, we can also determine the numerological influences of months and days as they relate to our birthdays. Numerologically, we experience nine-month cycles and nine-day cycles. Within the nine-year-cycles there are nine-month-cycles, and within the nine-month-cycles there are nine-day-cycles. These are our *Personal Months* and *Personal Days*. The number values of our Personal Months and Personal Days describe what we can expect during any given month or on any given day. Each Personal Month and Personal Day is part of a cycle of nine, and each has its own particular vibration. Each Personal Month describes how best to approach activities during the month as well as how to make the most of your Personal Year vibrations during that particular month. Each Personal Day describes the influences of any particular day and, like Personal Months, they should be interpreted in the context of the Personal Month. Like Personal Years, the influences of the Personal Months and Personal Days trump the influences of the Universal Months and Universal Days.

Calculating Your Personal Month

Like Personal Years, Personal Months and Personal Days are simple to calculate. In addition to the numbers *1* through *9*, I use the master numbers *11* and *22*. To find your Personal Month Number, add the current or Universal Month Number to your Personal Year Number.

For example, let's assume (again) that you were born April 20, 1986 and the current date is January 3, 2011. Your Personal Year Number is *9* (Birth Day + Birth Month + Current Year = 20 + 4 + 2011 = 1). The current or Universal Month Number is January, the 1st month of the year. Add the number of the Universal Month to the number of your Personal Year. 1 + 1 = 2. Your Personal Month Number is *2* (written 2-Personal-Month).

Birthdate: April 20, 1986
Universal Date: January 3, 2011
Universal Month: January (the 1st month)
Personal Year: 1
Personal Month: 1 + 1 = 2
The Personal Month number is *2* (written *2-Personal-Month*).

Birthdate – April 20, 1986/Universal Date – January 3, 2011										
Birth Month	April	=	4	=	4	=	4			
Birth Day	20	=	20	=	2 + 0	=	2			
Current Year	2011	=	2011		2 + 0 + 1 +1	=	4			
Personal Year					4 + 2 + 4	=	10	=	1 + 0 = 1	
Current Month	January	=	1	=	1	=	1	=	1	
Total									1 + 1	
Reduced Total									1 + 1	=	2

Let's do another (again).

Birthdate: May 13, 1973
Universal Date: August 11, 2010
Universal Month: August (the 8th month)
Personal Year: 3
Personal Month: 3 + 8 = 11

To find your Personal Month, add the Universal Month to your Personal Year. Your Personal Year is *3* (Birth Day + Birth Month + Current Year = 13 + 5 + 2010 = 3). The Universal Month is August, the 8th month of the year. Add the number of the Universal Month to the number of your Personal Year. 8 + 3 = 11.

Your Personal Month number is *11* (written *11-Personal-Month*).

Birthdate – May 13, 1973/Universal Date – August 11, 2010								
Birth Month	May	=	5	=	5	=	5	
Birth Day	13	=	13	=	1 + 3	=	4	
Current Year	2010	=	2010		2 + 0 + 1 + 0	=	3	
Personal Year					5 + 4 + 3	=	12 = 1 + 2	3
Current Month	August	=	8	=	8	=	8	8
Total								11
Reduced Total					Do Not Reduce			11

Let's do another.

Birthdate: December 18, 2001
Current Year: November 28, 2009
Birth Day: 18
Birth Month: December
Personal Year: 12 + 18 + 2009 = 5
Universal Month: November (the 11th month)
Personal Month: 11 + 5 = 16 = 1 + 6 = 7

Add the Universal Month to your Personal Year. Your Personal Year is *5* (Birth Day + Birth Month + Current Year = 18 + 12 + 2009 = 5). The Universal Month is November, the 11th month of the year. Add the number of the Universal Month to the number of your Personal Year. 11 + 5 = 16. Reduce to a single digit or master number. 16 = 1 + 6 = 7.

Your Personal Month number is *7* (written *7-Personal-Month*).

Birthdate – April 20, 1986/Universal Date – January 3, 2011										
Birth Month	December	=	12	=	1 + 2	=	3			
Birth Day	18	=	18	=	1 + 8	=	9			
Current Year	2009	=	2009	=	2 + 0 + 0 + 9	=	11			
Personal Year					3 + 9 + 11	=	23	=	2 + 3 = 5	
Current Month	November	=	11	=	11	=	11	=	11	
Total									16	

Reduced Total											$1 + 6 =$	7

Meanings of the Personal Month

Personal Month 1

A 1-Personal-Month is the month for new beginnings—a perfect time to begin a new project, make a fresh start, or try on a new attitude. If you have been putting off starting a new job, taking a new class, or joining a gym, this is the time to stop thinking and start doing. This month emphasizes independence, individuality, initiative, novelty, self-reliance, spontaneity, and variety. The focus is on you and your aspirations. Let your sense of selfhood (who you think you are) develop and expand as you face novel ideas and situations. Develop new skills and talents, invest in yourself, and follow your dreams. Take a chance, welcome new opportunities. This month gives you opportunities to demonstrate action, creativity, and originality. Some may be called on to act in a leadership capacity. This month usually brings with it good health and a high energy level.

Personal Month 2

This month emphasizes an increasing awareness of others, an interest in relationships of all kinds, and a time to take into account the needs, desires, and motivations of others. Partnerships, lovers and friends, competitors and enemies take on added significance. You will become more aware of how others may be helpful or hurtful. Your greatest progress will come from being a part of a couple or a team. Adaptability, adjustment, cooperation, diplomacy, and receptivity will further your interests. Career and finances may move slowly. You may even experience some lows in regards to vitality and energy. Some may find need to give their attention to their home or parents, especially your mother or maternal figures. Some may need to address the public about a concern or project. This month does not favor personal concerns, but it can favor romance and your ability to give and take on a more intimate level.

Personal Month 3

The 3-Personal-Month brings with it the potential for fulfillment, happiness, and joy. This could be a very social month for you—dates, parties, social gatherings, and group activities. Relationships and shared pleasures are characteristic of this month. Friends, partners, lovers, spouses, and fiancés as well as more casual acquaintances are emphasized. You may find yourself feeling more sociable and outgoing than usual. Your energies and interests blend harmoniously with those around you. Creativity, affection, imagination, inspiration, and self-expression are highlighted. Some of your dreams and ambitions may be fulfilled this month. You may get involved with the arts, music, or acting, or develop new skills and talents. Romance and finances are favored during a 3-Personal-Month.

Personal Month 4

A 4-Personal-Month is typically a busy one. You should give some form of concrete expression to your dreams, hopes, and wishes. This is a month of actions, challenges, restrictions, and obstacles, and it requires concentration, discipline, organization, patience, perseverance, hard work, and attention to details. Some form of crisis may push you to overcome personal limitations. This is a month of creative tension and possible confrontations. You could be challenged in one or more major life-arenas—home, health, relationships, work, or finances. Your responsibilities may increase temporarily, and your self-confidence may waver at times. Budgets and schedules may be helpful. If you put forth the effort to meet these challenges, you have much to gain this month and your sense of personal power will increase. However, be kind to your body and don't overwork. Good health is essential to getting the most out of this month.

Personal Month 5

A 5-Personal-Month releases you from the responsibilities, challenges, and struggles of the previous month. The pace of this month is rapid and largely unencumbered. This month brings change, excitement, enthusiasm, novelty, spontaneity, and variety with a pinch of restlessness. There are new opportunities to investigate, new people to meet, and new freedoms to experience. Expect the unexpected. Flexibility is an important prerequisite to getting the most out of this month, much less make progress. A 5-Personal-Month is for traveling and for taking chances. You can express yourself in a more unique and creative manner. Your thoughts, feelings, and actions may not be accepted immediately by others. This is a good month to promote yourself. Follow the new, but don't abandon the old. Try to temper any extremes with a little moderation. Career, finances, and relationships will benefit if you integrate the new with the old.

Personal Month 6

A successful and satisfactory 6-Personal-Month depends on the structures you built and the issues you faced during the 4-Personal-Month—family, home, love, career, finances, community. These issues return, but instead of the struggles, challenges, and confrontations of the 4-Personal-Month, you will receive the fruits of your actions during the 4-Personal Month. What was built or what was faced during the 4-Personal-Month bears fruit. The 6-Personal-Month is a time for enjoying your success, productivity, relationships, and harmony. This is a month of optimism, understanding, justice, and reciprocation. The more you give the more you will receive. Your morale is high. A 6-Personal-Month is much like the 3-Personal-Month—you will tend to find yourself surrounded by the best in friends, family, beauty, health, food, and everyday luxuries. All the resources that you need will be available to you as long as you take your responsibilities and duties seriously. New opportunities may sprout from what you have already accomplished. Vocational and financial matters tend to go well, as do interpersonal relationships. This is a good month for domestic conditions, marriage, and weddings.

Personal Month 7

Your 7-Personal-Month is a time for withdrawing from outer activities. It is a month for thoughtfulness, introspection, meditation, self-examination, and deliberation. During your 7-Personal-Month you step back from all that you have accomplished during the previous six months. It is a time to analyze and reflect on what you have learned about yourself and your world and to develop new insight and a new philosophy based on your recent experiences. Social activities may take a back seat to intellectual and/or spiritual pursuits. Some may maintain some degree of seclusion. There may be an interest in studying, reading, or specializing in some esoteric subject. The 7-Personal-Month can be a quiet time during which you may turn your thoughts towards self-improvement, idealism, and perfectionism. Your intuition may become usually active and sharp. This is a month for spirituality and religious concerns. You may find solutions and make important decisions this month.

Personal Month 8

Your 8-Personal-Month is the month for acting on the thoughts, ideas, and philosophies that you developed last month. You are testing the validity of the personal discoveries you made during your previous 7-Personal-Month. Many people are unaware that they are trying to actualize their new ideals. They are consciously aware that this month is one of intense, dynamic activity. You may need and desire to take specific actions which will further your goals. Your actions may be unusually individualistic, and you may display great vision, deep insights, and increased personal power. This month may emphasize money, finances, and material needs as well as advancements, promotions, and leadership. The 8-Personal-Month can be one of energetic activities, expressions of power, material accomplishments, and purposeful actions. You will need to be organized and efficient. Your interests are expanded, obstacles are overcome, and limitations are transcended. Broad comprehension and good judgment can lead to expanding business opportunities, making new investments, and signing favorable contracts. Enterprises and work involving corporations are favored. Recognition and publicity are yours if you want them. This can be a good month for career and finances. It does not usually favor intimate relationships.

Personal Month 9

The 9-Personal-Month is a good time for completing projects and endeavors of all types. This is not the month to start anything new. Endings, transformation, rebirth, and recycling are key themes this month. It is a month for subjective progress and growth and for the elimination of what is no longer useful. It is a good time for performing selfless service or promoting brotherhood and universal love. By cultivating an attitude that fosters love, compassion, tolerance, detachment, and selflessness, you will be rewarded with increased love, wisdom, understanding, and insights. The 9-Personal-Month can be one of spiritual understanding and Self-realization. This may be a time of endings, saying goodbye, and letting go. It is possible that a relationship may end during a 9-Personal-Month, or some similar loss may result in grief or sorrow. Your own energy level may not be as high as you desire.

Personal Month 11

The 11-Personal-Month can be one of great creative, religious, or spiritual potential. Spiritually, this month emphasizes idealism, religion, mysticism, renunciation, and illumination. Your intuition and psychic perception may be heightened during this month. On a material level, this month favors invention and technical genius. You may be benefited by science, electricity, radiation, magnetism, aviation, space travel, computers, telephones and cell phones during an 11-Personal-Month. An 11-Personal-Month can also manifest as a 2-Personal-Month, emphasizing an awareness of others, an interest in relationships of all kinds, and a time to take into account the needs, desires, and motivations of others. Partnerships, lovers and friends, competitors and enemies take on added significance. You will become more aware of how others may be helpful or hurtful. Your greatest progress will come from being a part of a couple or a team. Tact, diplomacy, and cooperation will further your interests. On a more spiritual level, you can be capable of developing psychic abilities or spiritual healing. You could take up mediation and metaphysical studies. You may gain insights into spiritual evolution. Career and finances may move slowly. You may even experience some lows in regards to vitality and energy. While this month does not favor personal concerns, it can favor romance and your ability to give and take on a more intimate level. Much is nebulous and intangible this month. It is important to stay as grounded as much as you can in order to gain the benefits of this you. For some, this month can lead to increased fame if other facts are in place.

Personal Month 22

The 22-Personal-Month can be one during which you can achieve your highest goals and actualize your highest ideals. This month is potentially a month of self-actualization, self-mastery, and personal transformation. You may be able to demonstrate a masterful capacity to combine materialism and idealism, inspiration and practicality. You may turn abstract conceptions into practical creations. Projects undertaken during this month can bring about wide-scale improvements, possibly having regional, national, or even international consequences. The secret for making the most of this month is to keep in mind that your actions are to be performed for the good of specific groups, communities, or societies. It is possible that some of your actions are for the benefit of all humanity. Taking time to meditate or to develop your intuition is necessary in order to manifest the best of a 22-Personal-Month. If you do not hold yourself to the highest standards, your 22-Personal-Month will function as a 4-Personal-Month. If this is so, you can expect challenges, restrictions, and obstacles to overcome. Concentration, discipline, organization, patience, perseverance, hard work, and attention to details will be important.

Calculating Your Personal Day

To find your Personal Day number, add the current or Universal Day to your Personal Month number and reduce the result to a single digit or master number. We will use the examples above. If you were born April 20, 1986 and the Universal Date: January 3, 2008. Your Personal Month is *8* (Universal Month + Personal Year = 1 + 7 = 8). The Universal Day is the 3rd. Add the number of the Universal Day to the number of your Personal Month. 3 + 8 = 11.

Birthdate: April 20, 1986
Universal Date: January 3, 2008
Universal Day: 3
Personal Month: 8
Personal Day: 3 + 8 = 11

Your Personal Day number is *11* (written *11-Personal-Day*).

Birthdate - April 20, 1986/ Universal Date - January 3, 2008						
Personal Year	BM + BD + UY	4 + 20 + 2008	=	7		
Personal Month	UM + PY	1 + 7	=	8		
Universal Day	3		=	3		
Personal Day	UD + PM			3 + 8	=	11

Let's do another (again).

Birthdate: May 13, 1996
Universal Date: October 10, 2011
Personal Year: 05 + 13 + 2011 = 22
Personal Month: 10 + 22 = 32 = 3 + 2 = 5
Universal Day: 10
Personal Day: 10 + 5 = 15 = 1 + 5 = 6

If you were born May 13, 1996 and the Universal Date: July 10, 2011. Your Personal Month is *5* (Universal Month + Personal Year = 10 + 22 = 32 = 3 + 2 = 5). The Universal Day is the 10th. Add the number of the Universal Day to the number of your Personal Month. 10 + 5 = 15 = 1 + 5 = 6. Your Personal Day number is *6* (written *6-Personal-Day*).

Birthdate - May 13, 1996/ Universal Date - October 10, 2011						
Personal Year	BM + BD + UY	5 + 13 + 2011	=	22		
Personal Month	UM + PY	10 + 22	=	32 = 3 + 2	=	5
Universal Day	10	1 + 0	=	1	=	1
Personal Day	UD + PM					6

Meanings of the Personal Day

Personal Day 1

A day to promote your interests and accentuate your individuality. You may have an increased sense of well-being. A day to be assertive, original, and spontaneous. Take a chance, welcome new opportunities, start something new.

Personal Day 2

A day that emphasizes significant relationships and increases your awareness of the needs and desires of others. You gain the most by being part of a couple or a team. This can be a favorable time for romance. Competition or confrontations are possible. Express yourself with tact and diplomacy. Balance assertion and individuality with patience and cooperation.

Personal Day—3

A pleasant day and a good time for self-expression, creativity, and communication. This day is favorable time for socializing, entertaining, and enjoying the company of others. Today could bring joy, fulfillment, and happiness. Good for romance, taking chances, and financial gain.

Personal Day—4

Today emphasizes the practical and constructive sides of life. It is a day for building a solid foundation. A day that requires work, drive, organization, and scheduling. The use of energy or force to overcome an obstacle.

Personal Day—5

A change of pace and attitude. Transform any excessive, restless energy into creative insights, new ideas, mind expansion, travel, sports, or games. A time for changes, for the expression of personal freedom, for spontaneity, new opportunities, and going with the flow. Feelings of enthusiasm for life and a temporary, but well-deserved escape from responsibilities.

Personal Day—6

A day to return to your responsibilities. This day can be a very productive one. Success comes from a combination of skillful effort and available resources. Family, home, community, health, service, food, and everyday luxuries are emphasized.

Personal Day—7

Take time for yourself away from social engagements and most everyday activities. A day to withdraw, read a book, or meditate. This day stresses quietude, introspection, self-improvement, religious concerns, ideals, and spirituality.

Personal Day—8

Today is a day for energetic activities, expressions of power, material accomplishments, and purposeful actions. Goals are reached; obstacles overcome. This day emphasizes finances, money, investments, business, enterprise, and corporations. Good judgment can lead to signing favorable contracts, making wise investments, and expanding business opportunities.

Personal Day—9

A good day to complete projects and similar endeavors. A day of endings, saying goodbye, and letting go. Possibly the ending of a relationship. Loss or sorrow. A time for performing selfless service or promoting brotherhood and universal love.

Personal Day—11

A day with great creative, religious, or spiritual potential. Today emphasizes idealism, intuition, and illumination. This day favors invention and technical genius on the material plane and psychic perception on the spiritual plane.

Personal Day—22

This is a day for actualizing your highest goals and ideals. A time for taking action in order to accomplish your plans. You can demonstrate a masterful capacity to combine materialism and idealism successfully.

Birthpath Periods
Your Key Cyclic Vibrations
Chapter 6

Our great symbol for the Goddess is the moon,
whose three aspects reflect the three stages in women's lives
and whose cycles of waxing and waning
coincide with women's menstrual cycles.
Carol P. Christ

Events tend to recur in cycles...
W. Clement Stone

Everything goes in cycles, to a degree.
Herb Brooks

Numerology divides life into three periods called *Birthpath* or *Lifepath Periods*. Each period is a stage of life during which we are to develop a particular energy symbolized by the numerological value of that stage. Opening consciously to the numerological vibration of the period can be highly beneficial.

The numerical value of each Birthpath Period is determined very simply from the birthdate. The First Birthpath Period is determined by adding together the digits of the month of birth and reducing the sum to a single digit or master number. The Second Birthpath Period is determined by adding together the digits of the day of birth and reducing the sum to a single digit or master number. The Third Birthpath Period is determined by adding together the digits of the year of birth and reducing the sum to a single digit or master number.

The Timing of the Birthpath Periods

While determining the value of each Birthpath Period is simple, determining the beginning and ending of each Birthpath Period is a little more difficult. Each period lasts around 28 years like the cycles of the progressed Moon and transiting Saturn.

The First Birthpath Period begins at birth and ends at the end of the 9 Personal Year closest to the 27th birthday. The Second Birthpath Period begins on January 1st of the 1 Personal Year closest to the 28th birthday. The Second Birthpath Period ends at the end of the 9 Personal year closest to the 55th birthday. The Third Birthpath Period begins on January 1st of the 1 Personal Year closest to the 56th birthday.

The table below, based on the value of the Birthpath, gives the age ranges of the Birthpath Periods for each Birthpath:

Life Path Number	First Life Path Period	Second Life Path Period	Third Life Path Period
9	0 - 27	28 - 54	55 on
8	0 - 28	29 - 55	56 on
7	0 - 29	30 - 56	57 on
6	0 - 30	31 - 57	58 on
5	0 - 31	32 - 58	59 on
4	0 - 23	24 - 59	60 on
3	0 - 24	25 - 51	52 on
2	0 - 25	26 - 52	53 on
1	0 - 26	27 - 53	54 on

The Meaning of the Birthpath Periods

Birthpath Period 1

This Birthpath Period indicates a time of new beginnings, fresh starts, and pioneering firsts. Your unique individuality is emphasized. You will be called upon to express your initiative, spontaneity, independence, and self-reliance. Expect opportunities, novelty, variety, and adventure. You will be encountering new situations, circumstances, and relationships.

Birthpath Period 2

This Birthpath Period indicates a time that emphasizes partnerships and cooperation. Your capacity for forming and maintaining relationships is emphasized. You will be called on to provide others with support. Working with others and learning to compromise are necessary. You will need to demonstrate sensitivity, empathy, and sympathy. For some, this period can indicate marriage or a significant love relationship. It can also signify opposition from competitors.

Birthpath Period 3

This Birthpath Period indicates a time that emphasizes your social life and your ability to enjoy the good things in life. This Birthpath Period is generally a time to focus is on your own interests, needs, and desires. Happiness and fulfillment are within your reach. Romance is a good possibility.

There are opportunities to use your skills, talents, and abilities. Your efforts are rewarded. Communications in general and writing specifically are favorable now.

Birthpath Period 4

This Birthpath Period indicates a time of construction, challenge, and creative tension. This Birthpath Period is often an active, energetic one. You will be motivated to give your ideas, dreams, and plans some form of concrete manifestation. This is a time to build a power base and consolidate your strength. However, you should expect obstacles, confrontations, and crises. Hard work is necessary as well as concentration, discipline, organization, persistence, and patience. Although this period tests your character, skills, and abilities, it can also be a time of great achievement and accomplishment.

Birthpath Period 5

This Birthpath Period indicates a time of frequent and rapid change and transformation. This period brings a variety of new opportunities, new people, and new situations. You will need to be flexible, versatile, and spontaneous. This is a time to let go of the old and familiar. Some will experience anxiety and loss due to the changes this period brings. Others will welcome it as a solution to boredom and restlessness. You can discover new things about both the world and yourself. You may discover new interests, talents, and skills. This period is good for travel and relocation.

Birthpath Period 6

This Birthpath Period indicates a time of productivity, responsibility, and success. You are able to concentrate on the important structures you have built--your—home, family, relationships, career. When you fulfill your responsibilities and duties to others, your life will be filled with love, harmony, beauty, health, and luxury. The more you give the more you will receive. This period is good for marriage, weddings, finances, and vocation. Your morale is high, and you can expect a time of optimism, understanding, justice, and reciprocation. Your morale is high. While you will be making the most of whatever you have already accomplished, you will also be able to make the most of new opportunities. Vocational and financial matters tend to go well, as do your interpersonal relationships with friends, family, and co-workers.

Birthpath Period 7

This Birthpath Period indicates an unusual time of relative withdrawal and seclusion. You are able to further your personal and spiritual development by getting away from others. Some may be concerned or even obsessed with religious, metaphysical, spiritual, psychic, or paranormal topics. Spiritual or psychic development may seem highly important. For others, this is a period of intellectual, vocational, or technical specialization. Either way, this is a time for thoughtfulness, introspection, meditation, self-examination, and deliberation. You can accomplish much by staying away from typical social engagements. Your intuition may become usually active and sharp.

Expect life to be disrupted by the unpredictable, the irrational, and the karmic.

Birthpath Period 8

This Birthpath Period indicates a time of great material accomplishment. You will have opportunities to display your power, authority, and financial success. You express ambition, hard work, organization, and executive ability in business adventures. You may work with large corporations or governmental departments. This is also a time when you will encounter friction, frustration, obstacles, and limitations. Your stamina, skills, and abilities will be challenged. Your determination and persistence will be tested. Success does not come easily. You will have to be aggressive and competitive, but keep in mind that if others do not benefit from your services and your actions are not ethical, you will pay the price.

Birthpath Period 9

This Birthpath Period indicates a time when you can do great things for others. During this period you will have opportunities to dream big and follow those dreams if they involve the welfare of others. This is a humanitarian period when you can be recognized for your service to others. You can empathize with others and intuit their needs. You understand what needs to be done and can come up with solutions to significant social problems. You may function as a religious, spiritual, political, or community leader. However, you may not be without opposition or obstacles. Actualizing your dreams and projects may test your inner will. Forgiveness is important.

Birthpath Period 11

This Birthpath Period indicates a time of exceptional creativity and inspiration. You can be especially talented and artistic during this period. Your thoughts, ideas, and interests are likely to be quite unusual, and yet you are very willing to share them with anyone who will listen. Others will find you inspiring. You will tend to be more religious, spiritual, metaphysical, or mystical during this time.

Birthpath Period 22

During this Birthpath Period you will have opportunities to fulfill a collective or universal need. You may be quick to see solutions to complex problems. You can be most successful when you take charge of large-scale operations. Your actions may have global or universal effects. You are most likely to be constructive, responsible, and goal-oriented. You may be energetic, hard-working, and ambitious. You want to make a difference in the world. You will have opportunities to accomplish great things, especially in the arenas of politics, arts, humanities, industry, or business.

Pinnacles and Challenges
Life's Ups and Downs
Chapter 7

*You have reached the pinnacle of success as soon as
you become uninterested in money, compliments, or publicity.*
Thomas Wolfe

*Life's challenges are not supposed to paralyze you,
they're supposed to help you discover who you are.*
Bernice Johnson Reagon

*Opportunities to find deeper powers within ourselves come
when life seems most challenging.*
Joseph Campbell

The most popular numerological system for predicting future events and trends is the use of
Pinnacles and Challenges. However, unlike Personal Years, Months, and Days, Pinnacles and
Challenges refer to much longer periods of time. They describe general trends and the probable
nature of events, but they do not pinpoint the event dates. In numerology, the life span can be
divided into four periods called Pinnacles or Attainments. Pinnacles are nine-year cycles for
developing a particular numerological quality. It is believed that it takes nine years to develop the
numerological quality and reach complete fulfillment.

The four Pinnacles are roughly similar to the four stages of life described in Hinduism, to the dasas
of Vedic astrology, and to the Saturn returns in Western astrology. For example, the popular
vimsottari dasa system of Vedic astrology divides a 120-year life time into nine unequal periods of
time. Saturn returns divide the life span into periods of approximately 27 years. The durations in
these three systems are only roughly similar, and they may be combined to create more detailed
descriptions where their periods overlap.

The Pinnacles

The First Pinnacle starts at birth and ends somewhere around the ages of twenty-eight to thirty-five
years old, depending on one's Birth Path Number. The number or value of this Pinnacle refers to
the development of the ego and its personality. The Second Pinnacle covers the next nine years
and is a time that emphasizes productivity, responsibility, and family relationships. The Third
Pinnacle symbolizes the period of middle age and maturity. The Fourth Pinnacle describes one's
senior years.

There are two sets of calculations involved in using the Pinnacles. The first set of calculations
involves determining the beginnings and endings of the Pinnacles. The second involves

determining the numerical values, i.e., numerological values, of the four Pinnacles.

The Timing of the Pinnacles

The timing of the four Pinnacles depends on one's Birth Path Number. As mentioned above, the Pinnacles are based on nine-year cycles. The First Pinnacle is an exception, however, in that the length of the First Pinnacle is the sum of four nine-year cycles minus the Birth Path Number. That is, the First Pinnacle begins at birth; the last year of the First Pinnacle is determined by subtracting the value of the Birth Path Number from 36. The number 36 is the result of four cycles of nine years—4 x 9 = 36.

For example, if your Birth Path Number is 1, subtract 1 from 36. 36 – 1 = 35. For a person with a Birth Path Number of 1, the First Pinnacle begins at birth and ends at the age of 35-years-old. For person with a Birth Path Number of 2, the First Pinnacle begins at birth and ends at the age of 34-years-old. 36 – 2 = 34. When calculating the end of the First Pinnacle, all master numbers are reduced to single digits before they are subtracted from 36. There is no 36 – 11, 36 – 22, or 36 – 33. There are 36 – 2, 36 – 4, and 36 – 6.

The Second Pinnacle begins the year after the First Pinnacle ends and ends nine years later. If your Birth Path Number is 1, your Second Pinnacle begins at the age of 36-years-old and ends at the age of 44-years-old. Don't worry; there is a table below that simplifies these calculations.

The Third Pinnacle begins the year after the Second Pinnacle ends and ends nine years later. The Fourth Pinnacle begins the year after the Third Pinnacle ends and continues until death. Below is the table for quickly determining the beginnings and endings of the four Pinnacles based on the Birth Path Number.

The Beginning and Ending Ages of the Four Pinnacles

Life Path Number	Pinnacle Periods			
	First Pinnacle	Second Pinnacle	Third Pinnacle	Fourth Pinnacle
1	0 - 35	36 - 44	45 - 53	54 - Θ
2/11	0 - 34	35 - 43	44 - 52	53 - Θ
3	0 - 33	34 - 42	43 - 51	52 - Θ
4/22	0 - 32	33 - 41	42 - 50	51 - Θ
5	0 - 31	32 - 40	41 - 49	50 - Θ
6/33	0 - 30	31 - 39	40 - 48	49 - Θ
7	0 - 29	30 - 38	39 - 47	48 - Θ

| 8 | 0 - 28 | 29 - 37 | 38 - 46 | 47 - Θ |
| 9 | 0 - 27 | 28 - 36 | 37 - 45 | 46 - Θ |

Calculating the Numerological Values of the Pinnacles

The numerological values of the Pinnacles are determined from the date of birth. The First Pinnacle is found by adding together the day and month of birth and reducing it to a single digit or master number. The Second Pinnacle is found by adding together the day and year of birth and reducing it to a single digit or master number. The Third Pinnacle is found by adding together the First and Second Pinnacles and reducing it to a single digit or master number. The Fourth Pinnacle is found by adding together the month and year of birth and reducing it to a single digit or master number.

For example, if your birthday is July 2, 1993, the value of the First Pinnacle is found by adding the day—2—to the month—July or 7. 2 + 7 = 9. If your birthday is April 7, 1981, the value of the First Pinnacle is found by adding the day—7—to the month—April or 4. 7 + 4 = 11. Pinnacles include master numbers.

If your birthday is July 2, 1993, the value of the Second Pinnacle is found by adding the day—2--and the year—1993. 2 + 1993 = 2 + 1 + 9 + 9 + 3 = 6. For April 7, 1981, the value of the Second Pinnacle is found by adding the day—7—to the year—1981. 7 + 1 + 9 + 8 + 1 = 8.

The value of the Third Pinnacle for July 2, 1993 is the sum of the values of the First and Second Pinnacles—9 + 2 = 11. For April 7, 1981, the value of the Third Pinnacle is the sum of 11 + 8 = 1.

The value of the Fourth Pinnacle for July 2, 1993 is the sum of the month—July—and the year—1993. 7 + 1 + 9 + 9 + 3 = 29 = 2 + 9 = 11. For April 7, 1981, the value of the Fourth Pinnacle is the sum of April—4—and the year—1981. 4 + 1 + 9 + 8 + 1 = 23 = 2 + 3 = 5.

Interpreting the Numerological Value of the Pinnacles

Pinnacle Value 1

This Pinnacle Value provides opportunities to develop independence, individuality, and leadership. It is time to follow your dreams and realize your ideals. Ambition, creativity, and originality are emphasized. Your successes will be noticed. You may need to let go of worn-out relations and break with the past. You may feel lonely going it alone, but it is necessary for your personal growth. You will need to demonstrate courage, self-reliance, and self-sufficiency. Your spontaneity and uniqueness are attractive to weaker souls. Some may find you charismatic. Some may find you too smug, self-willed, or bossy. Don't give in to anxiety, criticism, or perfectionism.

Pinnacle Value 2

This Pinnacle Value provides opportunities to develop interpersonal skills, diplomacy, cooperation, and patience. Close relationships are emphasized. Support, sensitivity, and empathy are needed. You will need to learn how to work with others. You success depends on your ability to assist others. Learn to follow, forgive, and harmonize. You may need to understand the behavior of others and their underlying motivations. At its best, this Pinnacle can indicate very special relationships and experiences of increased intimacy. At its worst, you might have to give up power and recognition to those less qualified.

Pinnacle Value 3

This Pinnacle Value provides opportunities to enjoy the finer things in life. Your social skills contribute to your success. You can be more enthusiastic, optimistic, gregarious, and playful. There is a release from routine, responsibility, and discipline. There is support for expressing yourself through writing, speaking, or acting. Indulge your artistic talents and temperament. A new love interest or harmony in an existing relationship is likely.

Pinnacle Value 4

This Pinnacle Value provides opportunities for practical, constructive, and responsible efforts to accomplish your goals. Dependability, concentration, efficiency, and precision are rewarded. Logic, organization, technical skills, and attention to detail support your vocational achievement. You have the drive and ambition necessary to overcome obstacles.

Pinnacle Value 5

This Pinnacle Value provides opportunities to try out new things, to take chances, and to indulge your curiosity. You can be bold and daring. Welcome change, variety, and uncertainty; they work for you now. You are enthusiastic about new ideas, places, and people and quick to adapt to the new and unexpected. Investigate what is novel and cutting-edge. Originality is rewarded. Personal freedom brings satisfaction.

Pinnacle Value 6

This Pinnacle Value provides opportunities to exercise responsibility for the welfare of family members and to take care of others' needs. It is a time to enjoy success in conventional terms. Productivity, harmony, and domestic tranquility give you time to appreciate your position in life and fruits of your labors. You take on the role of a service provider or responsible caregiver, both professionally and personally. Others respect you.

Pinnacle Value 7

This Pinnacle Value provides opportunities to develop your mind in the search of wisdom and truth. You can benefit by pursuing a scientific education or by specializing in a particular field. You are able to analyze detailed facts and information and intuit the underlying connections among seemingly unrelated facts, events, and situations. You may find that it is necessary to spend a great deal of time alone in your pursuit of your career goals. You will have time for reflection and solitude.

Pinnacle Value 8

This Pinnacle Value provides opportunities to achieve the high goals you have set for yourself. Your drive is strong, and you may even experience incredible physical stamina. You can accomplish whatever you put your mind to. You are hard-working, organized, decisive, and ambitious. You have executive ability and good, financial sense. You are quick to take advantage of every opportunity. You may be money-oriented, practical, and efficient. You are able to make a success out of whatever you undertake. You may have opportunities to weal power, control, and authority.

Pinnacle Value 9

This Pinnacle Value provides opportunities to follow your dreams. You are inspired to make to the world a better place. You may direct your energy into producing much needed products and services, but you could also fulfill your destiny through volunteer work or community service. If other indications are present, you could become a community leader on a path towards increasing recognition and responsibility. Your success will be enhanced by developing a broadminded approach to life and by using your intuition to see the big picture.

Pinnacle Value 11

This Pinnacle Value provides opportunities to follow your dreams. Trust your intuition. You can be very creative now and produce truly original works. Your connection with your higher Self is clear. You may discover a gift or talent you never knew you had. You inspire others. You may pursue interests in art, spirituality, or parapsychology.

Pinnacle Value 22

This Pinnacle Value provides opportunities to do something great importance to others. You can fulfill a collective or universal need. You can make a difference in the world. You are capable of turning ideas and inspiration into something real and concrete. You will also be capable of great self-discipline. You can achieve great things whether physical, emotional, mental, or spiritual. Ethics, morals and justice are especially important now.

The Challenges

The Challenges indicate the obstacles that you will encounter during life. These must be met, accepted, and overcome for life to proceed harmoniously. The Challenges may indicate qualities or behaviors that you need to develop. They may describe your weaknesses or the hurdles that you will face in life. Some numerologists used a system that includes two Minor Challenges and one Major Challenge. Others use a system of four Challenges similar to the Pinnacles. I will use the second system here.

Like the Pinnacles, the numerological values of the Challenges are determined from the date of birth. Also like Pinnacles, the timing of the Challenges are calculated in exactly the same manner. But the similarities end there.

Unlike the Pinnacles, the Challenges are found by subtracting the various parts of the birth date from each other. Also unlike Pinnacles, Challenges do not include master numbers. Unlike all the other numerological values, the numerical values of the Challenges run from 1 to 0. That is, the value of a Challenge is never 9. Instead, there is a Challenge value of 0.

Calculating the Numerological Values of the Challenges

The First Challenge is found by subtracting the day of birth from the month of birth, or vice versa, depending on which has the highest numerical value. The difference is reduced to a single digit. All master numbers are reduced to a single digit. A master number can never be a Challenge.

The Second Challenge is found by subtracting the day of birth from the year of birth, or vice versa, depending on which has the highest numerical value. The difference is reduced to a single digit.

The Third Challenge is found by subtracting the First Challenge from the Second Challenge, or vice versa, depending on which has the highest numerical value. The difference is reduced to a single digit.

The Fourth Challenge is found by subtracting the month of birth from the year of birth, or vice versa, depending on which has the highest numerical value. The difference is reduced to a single digit.

For example, if your birthday is July 2, 1993, the value of the First Challenge is found by subtracting the day of birth—2—from the month of birth—July or 7. 7 -- 2 = 5. If your birthday is April 7, 1981, the value of the First Challenge is found by subtracting the month—April or 4—from the day—7. 7 -- 4 = 3.

If your birthday is July 2, 1993, the value of the Second Challenge is found by subtracting the day—2—from the year—1993. 1993 -- 2 = (1 + 9 + 9 + 3) -- 2 = 22 – 2 = 4 – 2 = 2. For April 7, 1981, the value of the Second Challenge is found by subtracting the year—1981—from the day—7. 7 – 1981 = 7 – (1 + 9 + 8 + 1) = 7 – 19 = 7 – (1 + 9) = 7 – 1 = 6.

The value of the Third Challenge for July 2, 1993 is found by subtracting the value of the First from the value of the Second Challenge—5 – 2 = 3. For April 7, 1981, the value of the Third Challenge is found by subtracting the value of the Second Challenge from the value of the First Challenge--6 – 3 = 3.

The value of the Fourth Challenge for July 2, 1993 is found by subtracting the year—1993—from the month—July—7 – (1993) = 7 – (1 + 9 + 9 + 3) = 7 – 22 = 7 – (2 + 2) = 7 – 4 = 3. For April 7, 1981, the value of the Fourth Challenge is the difference between the month—April or 4—and the year—1981. 4 – (1981) = 4 – (1 + 9 + 8 + 1) = 4 – (29) = 4 – (2 + 9) = 4 – (11) = 4 – 2 = 2.

The Timing of the Challenges

The timing of the four Challenges is identical to the timing of the four Pinnacles. The timing of the First Challenges is determined by subtracting the value of the Birth Path Number from 36. The number 36 is the result of four cycles of nine years—4 x 9 = 36.

For example, if your Birth Path Number is 3, subtract 3 from 36. 36 – 3 = 33. For a person with a Birth Path Number of 3, the First Challenge begins at birth and ends at the age of 33-years-old. For person with a Birth Path Number of 4, the First Challenge begins at birth and ends at the age of 32-years-old. 36 – 4 = 32. When calculating the end of the First Challenge, all master numbers are reduced to single digits before they are subtracted from 36. There is no 36 – 11, 36 – 22, or 36 – 33. There are 36 – 2, 36 – 4, and 36 – 6.

The Second Challenge begins the year after the First Challenge ends and ends nine years later. If your Birth Path Number is 1, your Second Challenge begins at the age of 36-years-old and ends at the age of 44-years-old. Don't worry; there is a table below that simplifies these calculations.

The Third Challenge begins the year after the Second Challenge ends and ends nine years later. The Fourth Challenge begins the year after the Third Challenge ends and continues until death. Below is the table for quickly determining the beginnings and endings of the four Challenges based on the Birth Path Number.

The Beginning and Ending Ages of the Four Challenges

Life Path Number	Challenge Periods			
	First Challenge	Second Challenge	Third Challenge	Fourth Challenge
1	0 - 35	36 - 44	45 - 53	54 - Θ
2/11	0 - 34	35 - 43	44 - 52	53 - Θ
3	0 - 33	34 - 42	43 - 51	52 - Θ
4/22	0 - 32	33 - 41	42 - 50	51 - Θ

5	0 - 31	32 - 40	41 - 49	50 - Θ
6/33	0 - 30	31 - 39	40 - 48	49 - Θ
7	0 - 29	30 - 38	39 - 47	48 - Θ
8	0 - 28	29 - 37	38 - 46	47 - Θ
9	0 - 27	28 - 36	37 - 45	46 - Θ

Interpreting the Challenges

Challenge Value 1

This Challenge indicates the need to develop your individuality. You need to develop your independence and originality. You need to discover what is unique about you and pursue it. You will be required to stand on your own. You may even to be required to take on a leadership role.

Challenge Value 2

This Challenge indicates the need to learn how to cooperate with others. You need to learn how to compromise and let others take the lead. You need to learn compassion, empathy and sensitivity. You may need to put others first. Close relationships become more significant. You may need to take care of someone.

Challenge Value 3

This Challenge indicates the need to focus on your social life. You will need to overcome any shyness, meet new people, and cultivate new relationships. Meet and mingle. Develop your friendships. Part of this challenge is to work on your social skills and conversational skills. Writing may be important. Develop new ways of expressing yourself. Communication is important. Give physical form to your imagination. Get creative. An additional part of this challenge is to develop latent talents.

Challenge Value 4

This Challenge indicates powerful obstacles to accomplishing your goals. There is much difficulty, work, or hardship. Things do not come easily. Your patience, stamina, and belief in yourself are challenged. Don't be discouraged. You must put your shoulder to the grindstone so to speak. Achievement comes at a great expense. Tests and trials build your character. Practicality and responsibility are important.

Challenge Value 5

This Challenge indicates problems with freedom and change. On the one hand, you may feel that you do not have the freedom you need to lead the life you desire. Restlessness, boredom, and disinterest make it difficult to focus on the good things in your life. You feel trapped by stubbornness, rigidity, and immobility. You are unable to express your individuality and uniqueness. On the other hand, he may feel overwhelmed by constant change, abrupt change, and/or extreme change. All your resources are used up by meeting these changes. You crave stability, strength, and support. You don't have the time, money, or energy to do what you want to do.

Challenge Value 6

This Challenge indicates difficulty establishing a stable, comfortable, and harmonious home life. Your actions do not result in the desired outcomes. Productivity, commitment, responsibility, and domestic harmony are lacking. There is friction in relationships. You will need to learn how to replace authoritarian and similar distancing attitudes with love, service, acceptance, and appreciation.

Challenge Value 7

This Challenge indicates problems with elitist attitudes. Scientific or spiritual opinions and beliefs turn others off and cause separations from loved ones. Detachment and solitude are needed in order to come to more loving and inclusive beliefs. However, you may misuse time alone and reclusiveness to maintain and protect yourself. Others see you as critical and reserved. You need to embrace unconditional love. There is a spiritual crisis. You may need to deepen your knowledge and talents in a specific discipline. Mysteriously fated meetings, relationships, and coincidences can lead you either to your salvation or to greater misery.

Challenge Value 8

This Challenge indicates problems with the pursuit of money, status and power. Attainment, recognition, and enterprise are on trial. Accumulation of wealth is problematic. Numerous delays and obstacles to achieving your goals and ambitions will appear. You will need to work on your timing and organizational abilities. Planning, judgment, management, force, and hard work are important, but frustration is still inevitable.

Challenge Value 0

This Challenge indicates either the presence of all Challenges, the absence of all Challenges, or the opportunity to consciously choose the Challenge you want to tackle. During this period you have the skills and abilities of all the other Challenges within your grasp. You may be faced with many or all Challenges at once. You may also experience a time of peace and serenity. For some, this is the Challenge of choice. You must analyze your situation carefully and act wisely.

1 Plus 1 Equals 2, or Does It?
What Does Numerology Say about Your Relationships?
Chapter 8

Love looks not with the eyes, but with the mind;
And therefore is wing'd Cupid painted blind:
Nor hath Love's mind of any judgement taste;
Wings and no eyes figure unheedy haste:
And therefore is Love said to be a child,
Because in choice he is so oft beguiled.
William Shakespeare

From forth the fatal loins of these two foes
A pair of star-cross'd lovers take their life;
Whose misadventur'd piteous overthrows
Doth with their death bury their parents' strife.
William Shakespeare

Love is like a Rubix Cube,
there are countless numbers of wrong twists and turns,
but when you get it right, it looks
perfect no matter what way you look at it
Brian Cramer

Although numerology is one of the easiest of the metaphysical sciences to learn and apply, it approaches the complexity of the other forms of divination when it comes to relationships and compatibility.

In *Romeo and Juliet*, Shakespeare attributed love to the stars. In *A Midsummer's Night Dream*, he blamed the fairies. The fairy Puck summed up the mysteries of human attraction as "Lord, what fools these mortals be!"

While our initial attraction to someone may seem simple and obvious, it never really is. A relationship is a complex and complicated thing. So it takes complex concepts and complicated models to understand relationships.

Below is the relationship diagram used by Eric Berne, the originator of Transactional Analysis. Berne created this diagram early in his work. It illustrates the possible transactions from one person's first-order ego states to the first-order ego states of another. Between the three ego states—Parent, Adult, and Child—of the first person Bill and the three ego states of the second person Nancy, there exist nine possible types of complementary transactions.

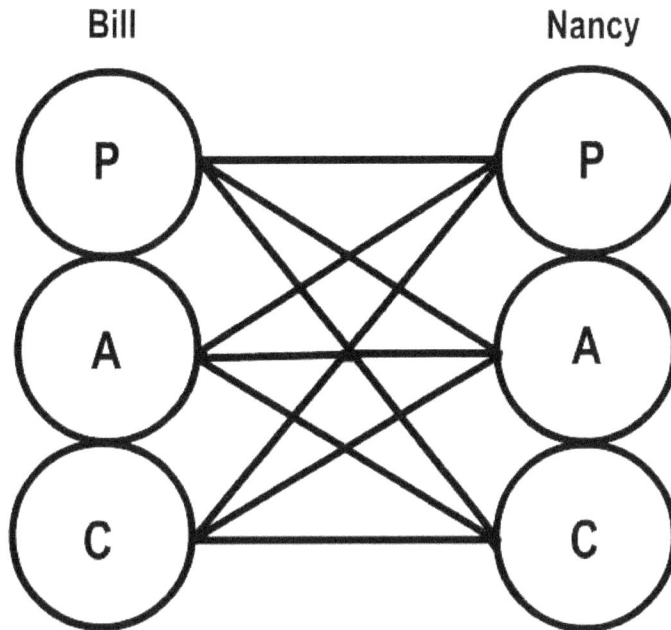

The Relationship Diagram

In actual practice, a transactional analyst works with second-order and third-order structural and functional ego states as well as crossed, angular, and ulterior transactions, resulting in quite a few possible combinations.

Psychology teaches that our relationship issues grow out of our early interactions with our primary care-givers. Our relationships offer the best avenues for healing our emotional wounds. Metaphysics teaches that our relationship issues grow out of our interactions with others in past lives. Our relationships offer the best avenues for healing our karmic wounds. Attending to our relationship-related lessons consciously opens the heart chakra and heals the root, sacral, and solar plexus chakras.

Using numerology to determine relationship compatibility requires an understanding of the qualitative meaning of the numbers, the relationships among the numbers, the , and the purpose or nature of the relationship.

Detailed and in depth, our relationship compatibility report compares each of the core numbers and tells you about your relationship. It also suggests how to avoid pitfalls and roadblocks. Accurate and insightful, the reports also serves as forecast detailing your cycles and trends for the coming year.

The reports gets into the Life Path number which gives a broad-brush outline of the relationship. This is derived from your birth dates.

The match up of your Destiny or Expression number relates to your goals and orientation in life, and determines if these are in harmony. This is the analysis that is based on all of the letters in your names converted to their number value.

It cover the matchup of the Soul Urge (the vowels in the names) and Personality or as we dub it, inner dreams (the consonants in the names).

The final segment of the reading is an important analysis of the Personal Year number which is so important in any relationship as it relates to what is happening this year and what to expect next year.

This reading is written by Hans Decoz, and it will be personally prepared by Michael McClain. Be assured there is no finer analysis on the market today. The reading is offered to Astrology-Numerology.com visitors for the very low price of $14.95.

1s in Relationship

1 – 1 The number 1 symbolizes individuality, independence, originality, uniqueness, and possibly leadership. It describes a relationship between two great individuals who admire and encourage one another. This relationship is very likely to be brief. It can easily turn into competition, power plays, hostility, antagonism, or indifference. It can only be maintained on a long-term basis if there are compatibilities between numbers on other levels.

1 – 2 The number 1 symbolizes individuality, independence, originality, uniqueness, and possibly leadership. The number 2 symbolizes opposition, awareness, and union. This combination describes the relationship between a leader and a follower. It can be very successful in accomplishing a variety of shared goals. It can be maintained over long periods of time. Much depends on the emotional development of the 2. It can stunt the growth of the 2 if it is time for the 2 to make significant changes.

1 – 3 The number 1 symbolizes individuality, independence, originality, uniqueness, and possibly leadership. The number 3 symbolizes synthesis, balance, and harmony. Both numbers are odd or masculine numbers. This combination can be very favorable for both persons. The 1 and the 3 work very well together.

1 – 4 The number 1 symbolizes individuality, independence, originality, uniqueness, and possibly leadership. The number 4 symbolizes construction, accomplishment, crisis, hardship, and challenge. Even though the 1 is an odd number and the 4 is an even number, this combination can be very successful as long as they respect each other for their differences. Both the 1 and the 4 are doers, but they approach life from very different mindsets. The 1 needs to accomplish things on his own, and the 4 needs to meet challenges in ways that create lasting results.

1 – 5 The number 1 symbolizes individuality, independence, originality, uniqueness, and possibly leadership. The number 5 symbolizes change, freedom, ingenuity, and restlessness. Both numbers

are odd or masculine numbers. This combination can be favorable for both persons. They share similar energies, interests, and activities.

1 – 6 The number 1 symbolizes individuality, independence, originality, uniqueness, and possibly leadership. The number 6 symbolizes productivity, cooperation, and responsibility. Even though the 1 is an odd number and the 6 is an even number, this combination can be somewhat successful. The 1 and the 6 have different skills and interests, and each can benefit from one another's strengths. They may live somewhat separate lives. Much depends on the compatibilities between their numbers on other levels.

1 – 7 The number 1 symbolizes individuality, independence, originality, uniqueness, and possibly leadership. The number 7 symbolizes consciousness, spirituality, sanctity, and specialization. Even though both the 1 and the 7 are odd numbers, they are otherwise quite different. They may be drawn together by their differences. However, this is normally a brief relationship, and they will soon be repulsed by these same differences. A healthy and harmonious relationship will depend on the compatibilities between numbers on other levels

1 – 8 The number 1 symbolizes individuality, independence, originality, uniqueness, and possibly leadership. The number 8 symbolizes organization, management, and power as well as friction, frustration, and adjustment. Even though the 1 is an odd number and the 8 is an even number, this combination can be somewhat successful. The 1 and the 8 have some similar skills and interests. They can benefit one another in the short-term. A longer relationship depends on the compatibilities between their numbers on other levels.

1 – 9 The number 1 symbolizes individuality, independence, originality, uniqueness, and possibly leadership. The number 9 symbolizes completion, compassion, devotion, and generosity. Even though both the 1 and the 9 are odd numbers, they are otherwise quite different. They are not likely to be drawn together. A short-term relationship of pupil and teacher might work. A long-term relationship will depend on the compatibilities between numbers on other levels.

1 – 11 The number 1 symbolizes individuality, independence, originality, uniqueness, and possibly leadership. The number 11 symbolizes intuition, illumination, inspiration, idealism, and talent. Both the 1 and the 9 are odd numbers and share many similarities. A short-term relationship will work well. A long-term relationship will depend on the compatibilities between numbers on other levels or on whether or not the 11 becomes a 2.

1 – 22 The number 1 symbolizes individuality, independence, originality, uniqueness, and possibly leadership. The number 22 symbolizes self-mastery and great accomplishments. Although the 1 is an odd number and the 22 is an even number, there are certain similarities that may establish a short-term relationship. A long-term relationship will depend on the compatibilities between numbers on other levels or on whether or not the 22 becomes a 4.

2s in Relationship

2 – 2 The number 2 symbolizes opposition, awareness, and union. It describes a relationship between two followers. It is not likely that two 2s will connect on their own. They may be brought

together by other circumstances. Whether or not they appreciate and value what they find in one another will depend on many factors, especially on their particular stages of growth. This combination can function quite well in certain circumstances. Much depends on the compatibilities between numbers on other levels.

2 – 3 The number 2 symbolizes opposition, awareness, and union. The number 3 symbolizes synthesis, balance, and harmony. Even though the 2 is an even number and the 3 is an odd number, this combination can be somewhat successful. This is not likely to be an exciting relationship, but it can be an otherwise successful relationship. In fact, it can be quite productive, comfortable, and growth-promoting. Much depends on the compatibilities between numbers on other levels.

2 – 4 The number 2 symbolizes opposition, awareness, and union, and the number 4 symbolizes construction, accomplishment, crisis, hardship, and challenge. Since both 2 and 4 are odd numbers, they should do well together. Much like a 1 and a 2, if the 2 plays a supportive role in the background, this combination can be very successful. However, the personal growth of the 2 will be restricted to this one role.

2 – 5 The number 2 symbolizes opposition, awareness, and union, and the number 5 symbolizes change, freedom, ingenuity, and restlessness. Since the 2 is an even number and the 5 is an odd number, they are not readily compatible. There is considerable incompatibility between the 2 and the 5. The 5 seeks change, variety, and freedom, while the 2 seeks relationship and balance. The 2 is in for a wild ride. Compare the numbers at other levels to determine whether or not this combination has any future.

2 – 6 The number 2 symbolizes opposition, awareness, and union, and the number 6 symbolizes productivity, cooperation, and responsibility. Both are even numbers and are compatible. This combination can be very productive and successful. Domestic happiness and stability are likely.

2 – 7 The number 2 symbolizes opposition, awareness, and union, and the number 7 symbolizes consciousness, spirituality, sanctity, and specialization. Since the 2 is an even number and the 7 is an odd number, they are not readily compatible. The 2 seeks relationship, and the 7 seeks to be alone. If the 2's needs for relationship are minimal or met elsewhere, a relationship may be possible. Much depends on the compatibility of the numbers on other levels.

2 – 8 The number 2 symbolizes opposition, awareness, and union, and the number 8 symbolizes overcoming problems and frustrations through organization, management, and power. Both are even numbers and are compatible. The 2 can be very helpful to the 8's ambitions.

2 – 9 The number 2 symbolizes opposition, awareness, and union, and the number 9 symbolizes completion, compassion, devotion, and generosity. Even though the 2 is an even number and the 9 is an odd number, this combination can be somewhat successful. Some characteristics of the 9 approach those of the 2. Check the numbers on other levels to determine whether or not this relationship can last.

2 – 11 The number 2 symbolizes opposition, awareness, and union, and the number 11 symbolizes intuition, illumination, inspiration, idealism, and talent. Even though the 2 is an even number and the 11 is an odd number, these numbers have some similarities. If the 2's self-esteem is good, the 3

can support the talents of the 11. If the 11 fails to focus on his or her inspiration, the 11 can become a 2 and the relationship can become boring.

2 – 22.

1s in Relationship

3 – 3

3 – 4

3 – 5

3 – 6

3 – 7

3 – 8

3 – 9

3 – 11

3 – 22.

1s in Relationship

4 – 4

4 – 5

4 – 6

4 – 7

4 – 8

4 – 9

4 – 11

4 – 22.

1s in Relationship

$5 - 3$

$5 - 4$

$5 - 5$

$5 - 6$

$3 - 7$

About The Author

Gene F. Collins, Jr., Ph.D. has been counseling, consulting, teaching, and writing in the areas of astrology, numerology, tarot, meditation, metaphysics, psychology, psychotherapy, parapsychology, and transpersonal psychology for over 40 years. He has served as a clinical psychologist, mental health counselor, and psychotherapist in a variety of settings including major university, government, and private medical centers, psychiatric hospitals, and mental health centers in both Florida and Illinois. He is a retired licensed psychologist in Florida and a retired clinical psychologist in Illinois.

Dr. Collins received his B.A. in Psychology (1974) and his M.A. in Clinical Psychology (1975) from Bradley University, and his Ph.D. in Clinical-Community Psychology (1985) from the University of South Florida. He has published as a second author in *Developmental Psychology* (1975) and as a first author in the *Journal of Sex & Marital Therapy* (1984).

Dr. Collins is certified in natal astrology (1974), is a Life Advanced Member of the American Federation of Astrologers (LAMAFA), and has served as the Vice President of the Illinois Federation of Astrologers. He specializes in natal, predictive, psychological, and karmic astrology as well as relationship compatibility (synastry). He is the author of *Cosmopsychology – The Psychology of Humans as Spiritual Beings* (2009) and *Cosmopsychology – A Holistic Approach to Natal Astrology* (2011).

In addition to his clinical and community work, Dr. Collins has taught psychology, communications, relationship, and personal growth classes at both the undergraduate and graduate levels, and has been published in both professional journals and community magazines. His professional include personal growth, the psychology of romance, sex and marital therapy, sexual identity, transpersonal psychology, alternative medicine, AIDS, and death and dying.

Dr. Collins has advance training and/or certification in hypnotherapy, personality assessment, sex therapy, stress management, client-centered therapy, gestalt therapy, rational-emotive therapy, transactional analysis, crisis counseling, and telephone therapy as well as transcendental meditation, silva mind control, est training, and graphoanalysis. He has been a member of Expanding Human Awareness, the American Federation of Astrologers, the Illinois Federation of Astrologers, the Illinois Psychological Association, the American Psychological Association, the Southeastern Psychological Association, the Florida Psychological Association, the Association for Transpersonal Association, and the International Transactional Analysis Association.

CPSIA information can be obtained
at www.ICGtesting.com
Printed in the USA
LVHW101341110221
679064LV00032B/914

9 781460 981672